Civil War England

Longman Travellers Series

Civil War England

PETER YOUNG
Line drawings by Stephen Beck

Longman *London and New York*

Longman Group Limited
Longman House
Burnt Mill, Harlow
Essex, U.K.

Published in the United States of
America by Longman Inc., New York.

First published 1981

British Library Cataloguing in Publication Data

Young, Peter
    Civil War England. – (Longman travellers series).
    1. Great Britain – History – Civil War, 1642–1649
    2. Great Britain – Description and travel – 1971 – Guide-books
    I. Title
    914.2'04'857   DA415   79-42835

ISBN 0-582-50286-1

Set in 10/12pt V-I-P Palatino
Printed in Great Britain by
William Clowes Limited, Beccles and London

Contents

CHAPTER 1

For King or Parliament?

Kings are by God appointed
And damned are those who dare resist,
Or touch the Lord's Anointed.

The Vicar of Bray

Tho' the King's crown do hang upon a bush, yet I charge you
do not forsake it.
   Sir Thomas Wyndham, on his deathbed, to his sons. 1637

I judge a man by only one thing. Which side would he have
liked his ancestors to fight on at Marston Moor? That's all I
want to know about him.

Isaac Foot

Mr Foot spoke for me too – but he would not like my answer. To
my mind a king of very ordinary ability is better than a good
president. In the nature of things a president arrives at his high
office, by a series of shifts and manœuvres of a sort wholly
inappropriate in one destined to be the Fount of Honour in the
Nation. How much better that the Sovereign should be above the
maelstrom of political strife. That is the position in Great Britain
today. It was not so in 1625 when the young King Charles I
(1600–49) came to the throne. He was singularly ill-equipped for
his role, a small weak child, with an impediment in his speech, he
had only become heir-apparent on the death of his brother Prince
Henry in 1612. By the time he ascended the throne he had become
a good horseman and could hold his own in tennis court or
tiltyard. But he was so shy and sensitive that he would blush at an
immodest word. He had an ear for music and was a connoisseur of
painting. For all that he was a singularly unimaginative man,
though retentive of impressions. From a political point of view

AREAS SUPPORTING KING
AND PARLIAMENT, MAY 1643

Key

Areas supporting
the king

Areas supporting
Parliament

Towns & cities

Castles & fortified houses

Berwick

Carlisle
Newcastle
Durham

Bradford
Leeds
York
Hull
Skipton
Preston
Lathom house
Liverpool
Chester
Derby
Lincoln
Newark
Nottingham
Shrewsbury
Stafford
Lichfield
Leicester
Kings Lynn
Coventry
Peterborough
Worcester
Northampton
Norwich
Cambridge
Hereford
Banbury
Colchester
Raglan Castle
Gloucester
Oxford
Cirencester
Bristol
Bath
Reading
London
Salisbury
Basing-House
Farnham
Castle
Maidstone
Dover
Taunton
Wardour
Castle
Winchester
Portsmouth
Arundel Castle
Exeter
Lyme
Plymouth

his main characteristics seem to have been the obstinacy with which he clung to his own opinions, however weak his position; and his remarkable ineptitude in the selection of his ministers. To remark that he was an excellent husband and father is simply to say that a man who would adorn the peerage is not necessarily fit for the throne.

The causes of the Civil Wars were essentially threefold – religious, constitutional and economic. Take away one of the elements and you get no civil war. They were, of course, interrelated. Which of the three was the most important? Who can say? The modern historian, living in an irreligious age, would perhaps emphasize the economic aspects. He would point to the idea that the King should live of his own, and show that the influx of precious metals from the New World had led to inflation, and had reduced the value of the Crown's fixed income from land. England in those happy days was perhaps the most undertaxed country in Europe. But that, oddly enough, did not make men any more anxious to pay a tax, which could by any stretch of the imagination be regarded as unconstitutional. Take the famous Ship-money case. The need for a navy was as evident then as now, but in 1653 many a good Cavalier of the Civil War period supported John Hampden in his stand against the extension of the Ship-money writs to the inland counties. But the need for money to carry on the government was not in itself sufficient to bring about an uprising, even when it became involved in a constitutional question like this.

The attempt to impose the English Prayer Book on the Scots brought a much greater danger. Riots in Edinburgh, followed by the signing of the National Covenant, brought a constitutional clash between the King and his determined Scottish subjects. Obedience could only be imposed by an army – which existed only in the shape of trained bands. The King, lacking money to pay for an army for any length of time, was compelled to summon first the Short Parliament (13 April 1640) and then the Long Parliament (3 November 1640). The latter after executing Charles' chief minister, the Earl of Strafford (1593–1641), and imprisoning Archbishop Laud, gradually drove the King into a position where he felt compelled to quit his capital, and allowed the country to drift into war.

In this war the supporters of the Parliament were at the outset drawn from those who were, in matters of religion, either Presbyterian or Independent. The Roman Catholics, at least in

3

King Charles I, by Gerard Honthorst *c.* 1628. (*National Portrait Gallery*)

the North, were solidly Royalist, and those we would call Anglican made up a large part of the King's supporters. It is true to say that the King derived his support from the North, Wales and the West, and the South-west. The more populous and economically developed countries of the South-east and the capital itself were, generally speaking, controlled by Parliament. The first Roundhead Army of 1642 had a number of peers amongst its officers. Equally, something like 40 per cent of the members of the House of Commons supported the King.

Turning to more physical assets, the King had at first none of the important ports save Portsmouth – which was soon compelled to surrender – Newcastle and Chester. The fleet with the exception of a few small ships declared against the King, who had built it. It was an important asset for the rebels, but it was not sufficient to enforce a complete blockade of the counties held by the Royalists, or to cut their communications between Dublin and Chester, or Newcastle and Hamburg. Unable to meet the enemy in a fleet action the Cavaliers resorted to a kind of maritime guerilla warfare. They obtained large numbers of small ships which could slip across to St Malo with Cornish tin or trade between Hamburg and Scarborough.

The great arsenals of the country were in the Tower of London, home of the Board of Ordnance, and in Hull, base for the Bishops' Wars. Both were in the hands of Parliament. So also was the

ENGLAND IN THE FIRST CIVIL WAR

Key

🏛 Towns besieged or stormed

🏛 Other towns

🏰 Castles or fortified houses

Battles:
1. Adwalton Moor (1643)
2. Marston Moor (1644)
3. Nantwich (1644)
4. Hotpon Heath (1643)
5. Naseby (1645)
6. Edgehill (1642)
7. Cropredy Bridge (1644)
8. Chalgrove Field (1643)
9. Lansdown (1643)
10. Roundway Down (1643)
11. Newbury I (1643)
    Newbury II (1644)
12. Langport (1645)
13. Cheriton (1644)
14. Stratton (1643)
15. Beacon Hill (1644)

Berwick

Carlisle
Newcastle
Durham

1 Bradford
Skipton
Leeds 2 York
Preston
Lathom House Hull
Liverpool

Lincoln

Chester 3
4 Derby Newark
Shrewsbury Stafford Nottingham
Lichfield
Leicester

Coventry 5 Kings Lynn
Peterborough
Worcester Norwich
Northampton
Hereford 6 Cambridge
7 Colchester
Gloucester Banbury
Raglan Castle Cirencester 8
Oxford
9 10
Bristol 11 London
Bath Reading
12 Salisbury Basing-House Dover
Exeter Taunton 13 Farnham Maidstone
Wardour Winchester Castle
Castle Portsmouth Arundel Castle
14 Lyme
15 Plymouth

ancient fortress of Windsor Castle. There was no standing army in England, but even so it seems astonishing that the King should have failed to put these fortresses in safe hands.

There was a standing army in Ireland, but it was fully extended in suppressing the bloody rising of 1641.

Well, on which side did your own ancestors fight at Marston Moor? There is some chance that you can find out if you want to. In a recent TV series Gordon Honeycombe described his researches into his own family history. I was able to find him a Cornish ensign, John Honeycombe, who was in Colonel Jonathan Trelawny's Regiment of Foot in the Royalist Army. He was one of about 7,000 old Cavaliers, who after the Restoration made claim to £60,000 granted by King Charles II to 'His Truly-Loyal and Indigent Party'.

A List of Officers, 1663, gives the indigent Royalists under the names of their commanders, mostly colonels, but sometimes generals. It must be used with caution. Officers of two quite different regiments are muddled together under 'Lyndsy Earl'. Robert Bertie, first Earl of Lindsey (1582–1642) raised the Lord General's Regiment of Foot, whilst his son Montague Bertie, second Earl (1608–66) commanded the King's Lifeguard of Foot. Again we find under Sir George Lisle:

'York   Norbury Edw. Lieut. to Maj. Skirrow'

and under William Ayliffe:

'L & W   Skirrow Rob Maj. FOOT.'

The explanation is this. Skirrow served from 1642 to 1645 in the regiment of (1) Colonel Richard Bolle, and (2) Colonel (Sir) George Lisle. He rose from ensign to captain and was taken prisoner at Naseby. He came out again in 1648 and served as major to Ayliffe in the siege of Colchester. Despite pitfalls of this sort *A List of Officers* is the nearest thing we have to a Royalist Army List. The information it gives can be expanded with the names of those who were compelled to compound for their estates, or to advance money to the Parliamentarian government. The editors of the Calendar of the Committee for Compounding were more interested in financial than military detail, and the serious family historian will, therefore, probably do well to

Overleaf: The execution of the Earl of Strafford, King Charles I's chief minister, 1641. The nucleus of the Royalist party was the group of 59 MPs – the Straffordians – who voted against his attainder. (*Reproduced by Courtesy of the Trustees of the British Museum*)

THE TRUE MANER OF THE EXECUTION
Lieutenant of Ireland, vpon Tower hill, th

HYBERNIÆ PR

Execution des Grafen Thomæ von Stafford Statth

A. Doct. Usher Primat in Irland.   C. Der Graf
B. Rahts Herzen von Londen.   D. Seine an

THOMAS EARLE OF STRAFFORD, LORD
of May, 1641.

IS SUPPLICIVM·

A. Doctor Vsher, Lord Prim-
le of Ireland,
B the Sherifes of London,
C the Earle of Strafford,
D. his Kindred and Friends

in Irland auf oē Tawers.platz in Londen 12 Maj 1641.
Stafford.
inten ynd freünde.

consult the original documents. The Cavaliers who figure in the Calendar of the Committee for the Advance of Money are on the whole of a rather lower social status than the compounders. For other ranks a valuable source is the Quarter Sessions Records. At the Restoration many old soldiers of King Charles I, petitioned for the pensions awarded by the JPs at the Quarter Sessions to maimed soldiers and mariners. Sometimes they give an interesting précis of their regiment's history. These records still exist for Devon, Kent, Wiltshire and several other counties.

These are perhaps the main sources, but they can, of course, be supplemented from heralds' visitations, county histories, news-books such as *Mercurius Aulicus*, memoirs and diaries such as that of the invaluable Richard Symonds, who rode in King Charles I's Lifeguard long ago.

On the Parliamentarian side we have the lists in Edward Peacock's *Army Lists of the Roundheads and Cavaliers* (2nd edn, 1874), in Joshua Sprigg's *Anglia Rediviva*, Rushworth's *Historical Collections* and the *Journals* of both the Lords and the Commons. Very important is *The Regimental History of Cromwell's Army* (2 vols, 1940) by Sir Charles Firth and Godfrey Davies. The *Journal of the Society for Army Historical Research*, the *English Historical Review*, the *Cheshire Sheaf* and a hundred-and-one such learned publications, illuminate – albeit in a somewhat haphazard way – the dark byways of that Civil War, from which the democratic system under which we live today, ruled by the Sovereign and the two Houses of Parliament, emerged at the Restoration of 1660.

I would like to be able to tell you that my own ancestors fought for the King at Edgehill or at Worcester. I cannot do so, I see from a 'Pedigree of the Family of Young' (1840), which hangs on my wall that Sir John Young, Kt of Leny (Perthshire), born 1601 is 'represented by Betham [whoever he may have been] as a loyal Cavalier', but no record of his services has come to me. His son, David Young of Leny (born 1623) married Lady Jane Grey, daughter of Henry Grey, first Earl of Stamford (1599?–1673). Now he was Colonel of that Bluecoat Regiment of Foot, raised 1642, which was the backbone of the Roundhead garrison of Gloucester (1642–46), and he also raised a troop of horse in Essex's army of 1642. He got himself soundly thrashed by Sir Ralph Hopton at Stratton (16 May 1643) and if Clarendon is to be trusted on the point, did not distinguish himself. 'Their General, the Earl of Stamford, gave the example, who – having stood at a safe distance all the time of the battle, . . . as soon as he saw the day lost (and some say sooner) made all imaginable haste to Exeter. . . .' He declared for the King in 1659 and King Charles II treated him with favour. I hope he deserved it.

CHAPTER 2

The soldiers

Military history is about people.

General Sir Anthony Farrar-Hockley

It is not so difficult to work out the main lines of the careers of the leading actors: King Charles, Oliver Cromwell, Prince Rupert, Sir William Waller and George Monck are only a few of the leading characters who have attracted competent modern biographers. The lives of lesser players are in a way more interesting for an army is only as good as its battalion commanders. Unfortunately, we have very little autobiographical material from the 'other ranks' of the Civil War armies.

Cavaliers

King Charles (1600–49).   Whilst temperamentally unfit for high command King Charles had certain military qualities: a somewhat passive brand of courage; and diligence in the performance of routine business such as attendance at the Council of War. The Royalist victory at Lostwithiel, especially the second phase – the pursuit to Castle Dore – seems to have owed more to him than to his generals.

The King's movements during the war can be traced in *Iter Carolinum* and from *The Diary of Richard Symonds*, who rode in the Lifeguard throughout the campaigns of 1644 and 1645.

Prince Rupert (1619–82).   The career and character of Prince Rupert has still a fascination which those of more successful generals lack. He had a truly astonishing series of successes, and not by any means were all of them cavalry charges. Here are some of his chief exploits.

23 September 1642: Powick Bridge, which gave first blood to the cavalry of the main Royalist Army.[1]

2 February 1643: The storming of Cirencester.

April 1643: The siege of Lichfield Close, to which the Prince brought miners from Cannock, and where a mine was sprung for the first time in England.[2]

17/18 June 1643: The Chalgrove raid.

11 July 1643: Padbury Fight.

26 July 1643: The storming of Bristol, the second city in the kingdom.

18 September 1643: Delaying action against Essex at Aldbourne Chase.

20 September 1643: First Newbury. Routs the right-wing of the Roundhead Horse under Stapleton.

21 March 1644: The relief of Newark, compelling the surrender of Meldrum and his army.

28 May 1644: The storming of Bolton.

7–11 June 1644: The siege of Liverpool.

July 1644: The relief of York.

22 April 1645: The routing of Massey at Ledbury.

On the debit side the Prince has been condemned – unjustly as I think – for being unable at Edgehill to follow up his defeat of Ramsay by a flank attack on Essex's infantry. He has also been condemned for his surrender at Bristol in 1645. It might have been possible to hold out for a time in the castle, but it would not, of course, have accommodated all the survivors of the regiments that had held the line, or all the horse. The court martial, held at Newark, which exonerated the Prince seems to have made the correct decision.

The worst blot on the Prince's military character, Marston Moor, is described in Chapter 8.

An excellent General of the Horse, Rupert was too young, and too lacking in tact to be Lord General of the main Royalist Army. Still, he was a thorough soldier: he took trouble to have an efficient staff, bringing experts with him from abroad: Bernard de Gomme the Walloon engineer and Bartholomew de la Roche. Though he was far from being a wealthy man he managed somehow to keep his own regiments of horse and foot well up to strength throughout the war. Many of the Cavaliers were men of an independent, fierce and unruly temper. They needed the

Prince Rupert, by Samuel Cooper (1609–72). (*Radio Times Hulton Picture Library*)

control of a strong leader of Rupert's brave and forthright character. There is a good modern life of Rupert by Patrick Morrah, and the Prince's movements during the war can be traced in *The Journal of Prince Rupert's Marches*, which was published in the *English Historical Review* for 1898.

Ralph, Lord Hopton (1598–1652). In my opinion Lord Hopton was the best of the Royalist generals. It is true that Clarendon thought him more fit to be the second-in-command of an army, than its commander-in-chief, but Clarendon was no soldier, nor was he with the Western Army during its victorious advance in 1643. He had, of course, the advantage of reading Hopton's account of his campaigns, *Bellum Civile*, which was written especially for him. But this you may also read for it has been published by the Somerset Record Society. It is a book which deserves to be much better known than it is, not only for what it tells of his own military methods, but because it is written in splendid seventeenth-century English and with a flair for detail. Hopton was an excellent disciplinarian. As a tactician he understood the use of ground and of weapons. He would have had little difficulty in adapting himself to the battlefield conditions of the Second World War.

A recent biography by an American scholar, F. T. R. Edgar, does not really do him justice. Only by reading his own account of his campaigns can one really assess this remarkable general.

Colonel Sir Henry Slingsby, Bart. (1602–58). Slingsby, who lived at Redhouse near the battlefield of Marston Moor, was a resolute Royalist, who was unjustly beheaded for his resistance to the usurpation of Cromwell. He was a serious-minded man as one can see from the diary which he kept for many years. Slingsby fought at Marston Moor and Naseby and gives us amusing sidelights on his campaigns, but practically nothing about the regiment which he commanded.

In this passage from his diary he gives his impression of King Charles during the weeks following Naseby:

> Here I do wonder at ye admirable temper of ye King, whose constancy was such y^t no perills never so unavoidable could move him to astonishment; but y^t still he set ye same face & settl'd countenance upon w^t adverse fortune soever befell him; & neither was exalt'd in prosperity nor deject'd in adversity; wch was ye more admirable in him, seing y^t he had no other to have recourse unto for councell & assistance, but must bear ye whole burden upon his shoulders; . . .

There is a good modern life of Slingsby by Geoffrey Ridsdill Smith.

Captain Richard Atkyns (1615–77).   Richard Atkyns of Tuffley, Glos., figures in the *Dictionary of National Biography* not for his soldiery, but for his writings on typography. Nevertheless, he served a campaign in Prince Maurice's Regiment of Horse and has left us a lively account of his doings. He fought at Little Dean (11 April 1643), and indeed gives the only detailed eyewitness account of that affair. Next he was at Ripple (13 April) of which, he tells us nothing save that he was in the forlorn hope under Major Thomas Sheldon, and that they did 'good execution upon the enemy . . .'. Then he was at Caversham Fight (25 April 1643) where he had much ado to keep his men from running, 'having a lieutenant as fearful an any; which to prevent, I was forced to cut some of them, and threaten my lieutenant; with which we stuck together more like a flock of sheep, than a party of horse'.

Atkyns was next in action at Chewton Fight, where he seems to have distinguished himself, and where his groom rescued Prince Maurice from captivity. Once more Atkyns' account is the most detailed that has survived. Of Lansdown (5 June) he says the 'battle was so hard fought on both sides, that they forsook the field first, and we had leave so to do'. He was an eyewitness next day of the tragic incident when Hopton was severely injured, and Major Sheldon mortally hurt by the explosion of the ammunition wagon. His account of Roundway Down (13 July) is largely concerned with his pursuit of Sir Arthur Hesilrige.

Prince Maurice offered Atkyns the major's place in his regiment, but he preferred, after the taking of Bristol, to return to his private condition.

Atkyns was perhaps no great soldier, but he wielded a fluent pen and his 'Vindication' gives us interesting sidelights on the character of the Cavalier Army.

Captain John Gwyn.   Gwyn was a better soldier than Atkyns, though by no means as ready with his pen. He came from Trelydan in Montgomeryshire, and could boast of his descent from Cadogan ap Bleddin, Prince of Powys and Brochwell, King of Powys.

Gwyn and five comrades joined Major George Boncle's Company in Colonel Sir Thomas Salusbury's Regiment of Foot at Brentford on 12 November 1643. This was a big regiment raised by the gentry of North Wales, especially Denbighshire, and Boncle, who Gwyn describes as 'our worthy old acquaintance' was probably its only officer of experience, the next being of the

W Sherwin *sculp*

Richard. Atkyns. Esq. Effigies.

Richard Atkyns. (*Reproduced by Courtesy of the Trustees of the British Museum*)

squirarchy of North Wales. Gwyn was soon made an ensign: 'I had the colours conferred upon me, to go on as I had begun.' Reading, Gloucester and the battles of Newbury, Cropredy Bridge and the defence of Devizes: these were some of the operations in which Gwyn took part. He is not always precise as to when the incidents he describes took place, but he certainly did not lack for adventures and narrow escapes.

> When a party of Waller's horse beat up our quarters at the
> Devizes, and furiously scoured the streets, giving no quarters
> to any soldiers they met, then I run and leaped across the
> street of such a sudden by them as to escape both their
> swords and pistols, when they killed Captain Jones, with
> others, and shot Ensign [Will.] Garroway in the neck.

On the surrender of Devizes Gwyn offered his services to Colonel Sir William Courtney, the Governor of Faringdon Castle, and though 'a stranger amongst those eminent soldiers' was given a company, and distinguished himself in a sortie, when, reading between the lines, he showed considerable tactical skill.

In the Second Civil War he was first captain in the Earl of Holland's Regiment of Foot, and was with the rearguard in the fight at Kingston, when Lord Francis Villiers was slain.

Gwyn was one of those soldiers who have never had enough. He went over to Scotland with the Earl of Kinnoul, during Montrose's last ill-fated expedition, and after many hardships got back to The Netherlands and was made a lieutenant in the Royal Regiment of Guards. He was at the siege of Ardres (27–29 August 1657), and fought on the Spanish side at the battle of Dunkirk Dunes, where, according to the Duke of York, afterwards King James II, after a stubborn resistance, the regiment, which was full of old Cavaliers, was compelled to surrender. Gwyn and a few others were particularly well treated by a Breton officer of Rambures Regiment, who offered them terms, for he and his escort after accepting their parole 'produced whole clusters of bottles of wine from under some of their cloaks . . .'. Not long after this Gwyn was given a company.

We owe Gwyn's rather muddled recollections of his military career, written about 1679, to the fact that after the Restoration he was given no command, but merely rode in the Royal Troop of Guards under the Duke of Monmouth. In his own estimation he should by right have been the major of the regiment, which is now the Grenadier Guards. But, wronged though he was, his philosophy was the brave old saying, 'What cannot be cured must be endured.'

The Royalist Army was full of such characters very few of whom left memoirs!

Bishop Peter Mews (1619–1706).   Mews, a Fellow of St John's College, Oxford, joined the King's Lifeguard of Foot – probably soon after the city fell into the King's hands – and is said to have received nearly thirty wounds on different occasions. In later life he always used to wear a black patch on one cheek of his decidedly forbidding countenance. He was taken prisoner as a lieutenant at the battle of Naseby, and forty years later he was in action once more at Sedgemoor. By that time he was Bishop of Winchester. During the battle he used his own carriage horses to draw the Royalist cannon to Feversham's right flank, and, directing their fire, received a wound from which he suffered for the rest of his life.

Mews was Vice-Chancellor of Oxford University (1669–73) and a very popular Bishop of Bath and Wells (1672–84). As visitor he supported the Fellows of Magdalen in their contention with King James II (1687–88). He also approved of the famous petition of seven bishops, but was prevented by illness from participating in their meeting.

Hospitable, generous and just, he was described by a contemporary as 'an old honest Cavalier'.

Peter Mews was not the only bishop who had fought for King Charles. Henry Compton (1632–1713), Bishop of London – and one of the seven – told James II in 1688 that he had formerly drawn his sword in defence of the constitution. He was the sixth son of Spencer Compton, second Earl of Northampton, who, scorning quarter, was slain at Hopton Heath in 1643. Northampton had regiments both of horse and foot, and the young Henry Compton, probably served in one or the other. It is not unlikely that he played some part in the defence of Banbury Castle – at the ripe age of fourteen! There were other Royalist officers of much the same age, and the future King Charles II saw his first battle, Edgehill, at the age of twelve. One does not think of 'Old Rowley' as a warrior king – yet as we shall see he acquitted

himself manfully at Worcester (1651), as befitted a grandson of Henri de Navarre.

Bishop William Beaw (1615–1705).   A fellow of New College, Oxford, Beaw left his studies and took twelve gentlemen, including some of his pupils and other scholars, into the King's service. Beaw

> served the King from a Pike to a Major of Horse, was wounded in the service (and on that account still halts) and kept long a Prisoner of war, and at last turned out of his Fellowship and all that he had, and forced by his sword (which at first he never intended to draw but for his own Prince) to seek his bread in foreign parts. . . .

He was a lieutenant-colonel in Muscovy, an 'honorable and profitable service', but left to join the exiled King Charles II, for whom he undertook many journeys by sea and land, and 'endured many hardships and often ran the hazard of his life for the space of above 2 years together, and all this out of his own purse . . .'.

His fortune spent, he served King Charles X of Sweden in his Polish Wars, and afterwards the King of Poland.

At the Restoration Beaw took holy orders and was restored to his fellowship at the King's command (30 August 1660). He was presented to the New College living of Adderbury, Oxfordshire (2 February 1661) and in 1679 Charles made him Bishop of

Llandaff, the poorest diocese in the country. Beaw, a friend of Henry Compton the Bishop of London, was like Mews a supporter of the seven bishops in their opposition to James II.

Richard Symonds (1617–c.92). Symonds, who came from Black Notley, Essex, served in King Charles I's Lifeguard of Horse during the campaigns of 1644 and 1645. He was present at Cropredy Bridge, Lostwithiel, Second Newbury, Leicester, Naseby and Rowton Moor. During all that time he kept a diary, which though it was published by the Camden Society about 120 years ago, is all too little known. Yet for a person wishing to visit the scenes of those two campaigns it is hard to think of a work which could be more useful. For Symonds was an antiquarian, and everywhere he went he made notes of the churches and their monuments, the leading families and particulars of that sort, as well as the composition of the Royalist Army and its movements. As one would expect, he is particularly useful for the doings of the Lifeguard.

Symonds says little of his own adventures, but there are indications that he played his part. Here for example is his brief account of a charge at Second Newbury (p. 145).

About . . . 4 of the clock, their bodyes of horse approached towards our field [Speenhamland, P.Y.] at the bottome of the hill neare the church called [Shaw], and one body came into our feild, [and] charged Sir John Campsfeld's regiment [The Queen's Regiment of Horse] which stood them most gallantly. The King's regiment being neare, drove at them, which made them wheele off in confusion, and followed them in the chase made all their bodyes of horse run in confusion, killed many, besides musqueteers that had lyned the hedges and played upon us in the chase till wee cutt their throats.

Of a fight at Huntingdon on 24 August 1645, where the Royalist cavalry routed some well-armed, but newly raised Suffolk horse, taking 100 prisoners, Symonds (p. 231) tells us little save that

Gosnal, Minor, Wroth, Sym. *et al. ceperunt*. They a little disputed Huntingdon, but wee entered, notwithstanding a large ditch encompassed it, lately scowred and cast up, and a breast worke and gate in the roads.

Theise rebells ran away to Cambridge; all of them back and breast, headpeice, brace of pistoll, officers more. Every troope consisted of 100.

Gosnal may possibly have been one of Glemham's officers, Rob. Gosnold, who was with that officer in the defence of Carlisle and later of Oxford. He came from Otley in Suffolk. Minors was probably Henry Mynors of Treago, Herefordshire. Henry Wroth, who was knighted on 16 September, became a troop commander in the Royal Regiment of Horse [Guards] after the Restoration. He came from Enfield, Middlesex.

It is not all that easy to obtain a copy of *The Diary of Richard Symonds* (see Select Bibliography) but to anyone wishing to follow the campaigns of 1644 and 1645 it is of the greatest value and interest.

Captain-Lieutenant George Reresby (d. 1646).   This officer was the son of Sir George Reresby. According to the Memoirs of Sir John Reresby he proved very wild, but a man of great courage and conduct in the late civil war. He might have had very good commands in the King's army, but contented himself with his first of Lieutenant to Sir Thomas Glemham's troop of horse under Sir Marmaduke Langdale, whom he accompanied in that famous raising of Pontefract siege, and got in it particular honour. Why he was not with Glemham at Carlisle does not appear. After the war he went to Thriberge and there died. He was buried in the church there on 6 July 1646.

Parliamentarians

Lieutenant-General Edmund Ludlow (1617–92).   Ludlow was born at Maiden Bradley, Wiltshire, the son of Sir Henry Ludlow, Kt, and Elizabeth Phelips, through whom he was related to the Royalist Phelips of Montacute. He was educated at Blandford and at Trinity College, Oxford, where he matriculated almost exactly 300 years before the present writer (10 September 1634).

Ludlow, who was a man of 'a gruff, positive humour', began his military career in 1642, serving for eight months in Essex's Lifeguard of Horse. He ran at Powick and fought at Edgehill. He then became a captain in a cavalry regiment to be raised by Sir Edward Hungerford for service in Wiltshire. Soon after he was made Governor of Wardour Castle and a captain of foot. It was not long before he found himself besieged, and although the place was not particularly strong he made a resolute defence. In his *Memoirs* he gives a very lively description of the siege, especially of a Royalist attempt to spring a mine and then storm. This took place about 10.30 at night.

'I was lifted up with it from the floor, with much dust suddenly about me; which was no sooner laid, but I found both the doors of my chamber blown open, and my window towards the enemy blown down, so that a cart might have entered at the breach.' The Royalists tried to climb up the rubble and in by the window.

> 'Those who stormed on my side were the Irish yellow-coats[3] commanded by Capt. Leicester. My pistols being wheel-locks, and wound up all night, I could not get to fire, so that I was forced to trust to my sword for the keeping down of the enemy, being alone in the chamber, and all relief excluded from me, except such as came in by me of my windows that looked into the court of the castle. . . .'

Mr Gabriel Ludlow organized his relief, but the ladder was nearly 2 yards too short, and Ludlow had to keep dashing across the room to help his kinsman climb in with his arms, and then dashing back to slash at the yellowcoats.

Compelled to surrender on 18 March 1644 Ludlow was soon exchanged, and on 10 May was commissioned as major of Sir Arthur Hesilrige's Regiment of Horse. Soon after he was made High Sheriff of Wiltshire. Waller gave him a regiment of horse, which, it must be said, did not do very well. It got off to a bad start on 6 July 1644, when Ludlow and the first 100 men he raised were routed between Warminster and Salisbury, and reduced to 30.

Ludlow fought at Second Newbury, where his cousin, Gabriel Ludlow, was horribly wounded, of which he died. 'This accident troubled me exceedingly, he being one who had expressed great affection to me, and of whom I had great hopes that he would be useful to the public.'

In December Ludlow was surprised by Sir Marmaduke Langdale at Salisbury, riding up by the Three Swans, he heard a great noise of horses in the street that leads in from Old Sarum. He went back to the market-place, where he found many Royalist

Edmund Ludlow. (*Reproduced by Courtesy of the Trustees of the British Museum*)

horse. Then he went 'by the back-side of the town-house through a street called the Ditch, to my guard, which was drawn up in the Close, but very short of the number I expected, . . .' some had gone to bed, others, under cover of darkness, had stolen away. In the fighting that followed, Ludlow fought with determination, but when the action was over he had lost about eighty more of his men. In April his major, Dowet, changed sides and took thirty men with him.

Ludlow was elected MP for Wiltshire (12 May 1646), and, though himself neither a Leveller nor an Anabaptist, associated himself from the first with the most advanced section of the popular party in the Long Parliament. He was one of those who brought about Pride's Purge in December 1648, was one of the illegal court which tried King Charles I and signed the death warrant.

In 1650 Ludlow was sent to Ireland as second-in-command, and so a brave, though scarcely successful, colonel became a lieutenant-general at a stroke. For nearly a year, after the death of Ireton, Ludlow actually held the chief command in Ireland.

Ludlow was opposed to the Protectorate, and Cromwell could not win his support. After the Restoration he fled abroad and lived most of his latter days at Vevey near Lausanne.

Sir Charles Firth summed up his character rather neatly when he wrote 'his faithful adherence to his principles compels respect, and his stubborn courage excellently qualified him to maintain untenable positions and lost causes'.

His *Memoirs* were published in 1698–99, but the publishers were far from being faithful to his manuscript.

Colonel John Birch (1615–91). Birch, whose ancestors had fought at Poitiers and at Agincourt, came of a family which had been established on the Lancashire–Cheshire border for 400 years. Before the end of the reign of Queen Elizabeth the family had become Puritan, and in the Civil War came out strongly for the Parliament. John was not its only member to distinguish himself. It was Colonel Thomas Birch of Birch Hall, MP for Liverpool throughout the Commonwealth and Protectorate that took the surrender of the Isle of Man from the Countess of Derby.

The Presbyterian colonel's 'martiall imployment' throughout the First Civil War is described in a military memoir, written by one Roe, who was either his secretary or quartermaster, which has recently served as the main authority for a fresh biography, whose title – *Roundhead to Royalist* – sums up his career.

Birch went to Bristol in 1633, prospered in the provision trade and married the widow of a grocer, who brought him a small fortune. According to Colonel Nathaniel Fiennes, his predecessor, Colonel Thomas Essex, had 'imprisoned Captain Birche, who is and always was the most active man in the town for the Parliament . . .'.

Roe's narrative begins with Prince Rupert's first attempt on Bristol (7/8 March 1643). It was he that raised the alarm, searched the houses of the Royalists, Yeomens and Bowcher, and robbed the Cavaliers of their Fifth Column.

When in July 1643 Rupert stormed Bristol, Captain Birch's post was on the southern sector, and he played his part in repulsing the assault of the Cornish infantry. After the surrender he sold up his merchandise as best he could and went to London.

Sir Arthur Hesilrige, who seems to have had some talent for selecting able subordinates, now made Birch lieutenant-colonel, and, in effect, commanding officer, of his regiment of foot.

Birch was with his new unit in Waller's surprise attack on Alton (12/13 December 1643) and led the assault on the church, where the bullet-marks made by his soldiers may still be seen.

> Nay (wrote Roe) at the entering of that church, dreadful to see the enemy opening the door, when ready to receive you with their pikes and muskets, the horses slain in the aisles of which the enemy made breastworks, the churchyard as well as the church being covered with dead and wounded amongst whom you long struggled, witnesseth the Lord's wonderful protection: from which day's service you escaped with a few dry blows with the musket stocks.

The Royalist commander, Colonel Richard Bolle,[4] was slain, but he is said to have killed seven Roundheads before he fell. Sixty of Bolle's men, it is said, fell with him, which argues a tough resistance.

The scene of this rough mêlée is not much altered, though a porch has been added to the church.

Birch was next in action at the siege of Arundel Castle, where he was severely wounded at the head of his men. As his secretary relates: 'The hand of God so assisting you that you kept in your guts, stopping the hole with your finger.' The surgeons thought him no better than a dead man, and, after their cheerful custom at that period, did not think it worth while dressing his wound. However the bitter cold of a winter night congealed his blood. . . . He made a fairly swift recovery, and was again in action at Cheriton, where he took a leading part in the recapture of Cheriton Wood.

Birch was with Waller at Cropredy and rallied the defenders of the bridge, when the Earl of Cleveland's charge had driven Middleton's men back across the Cherwell and taken eleven guns.

John Birch was at the indecisive second battle of Newbury, and in the pursuit thereafter pressed the Royalist Lord General, Forth, and eventually captured his Swedish lady, whose dignified self-assurance gave him his first hint that the loyalties of the Royalists were on a higher plane than his own. He rode back to Newbury with 57 prisoners and 128 captured horses.

After being in the defence of Plymouth, Birch took part in the offensive of the New Model Army, though his regiment was not actually incorporated in it. At Bristol his local knowledge was invaluable. He was put in Rainsborough's Brigade, and commanded the attack on Harnell Gate, which he took. His services were appropriately rewarded for in September 1645 he was made Governor of the captured city.

Birch had friends in Parliament, men of his own Presbyterian persuasion. In November he went to London and with their assistance got himself given orders to cooperate in the siege of Hereford. Its capture on 15 December was largely due to the skill and cunning with which he carried out his plan – which his secretary, Roe, records in considerable detail. On 22 December he was made Governor of the city, which he had surprised. This exploit was a turning point in Birch's career. He received the thanks of Parliament, who voted £6,000 for the payment of his soldiers. He was made Governor of Hereford, and chosen MP for Leominster, though he did not sit for long, being a victim of Pride's Purge (1648). Birch was rewarded with £50 per annum out of the estate of the Cavalier, Colonel Sir Henry Lingen.

Birch now went to work to fortify Hereford Castle so that 500 horse and foot could overawe the city, whose sympathies were strongly Royalist. The pulpit from which the Dean, Dr Herbert Croft, denounced the sacrilegious Roundhead soldiery (February 1646) may still be seen in the cathedral.

Birch was in the last battle of the First Civil War when Lord Astley's army was overwhelmed at Stow-on-the-Wold (21 March

1646). Here he had his horse killed and thirty-two of his regiment were killed, which shows what a desperate resistance was made by Astley's men, many of them reformado officers.

A few days later Birch had another horse shot under him in a reconnaissance of the Royalist fortress of Worcester. He was now ordered to summon Ludlow, whose Governor, Colonel Sir Michael Woodhouse, was notorious for his massacre of the Parliamentarian garrison of Hopton Castle. Sir Michael had served in Ireland. . . . He agreed to surrender Ludlow on 18 May 1646, insisting that he hand over the keys to Colonel Birch in person, 'expecting fair terms and performances out of knowledge of the said Colonel'.

Birch's last military operation was the siege of Goodrich Castle, stronghold of the enterprising and resolute Sir Henry Lingen, and key to Archenfield, that part of Herefordshire that lies between the River Wye and the Black Mountains. Its warlike inhabitants were strongly Cavalier.

The great mortar, 'Roaring Meg', which Birch used against Goodrich, may still be seen in the grounds of the Churchill Museum, Hereford. In the words of Alfred Watkins: 'We can picture the resourceful Birch getting his wooden pattern turned at some village wheelwright's with the lathe designed for the heavy waggon stocks. The site of the actual casting may have been the Old Forge, 1½ miles from the Castle, where the Garron Brook and River Wye meet the highway from Ross to Monmouth.'

Birch himself proved a skilful mortarman. He fired nineteen out of the twenty-two granadoes hurled into the place, and so accurately that every room in the castle was damaged. The defenders were reduced to firing stones from their 'hammer pieces'. Birch cut the water pipes leading to the castle, and its stone cisterns suffered from the bombardment. Mine and countermine in the solid rock paved the way for the final bombardment when, on 30 July, Birch's fire brought down the Ladies' Tower, blocking the countermine and laying the castle open to storm. Compelled to surrender with no better terms than 'mercy for their lives', the 170 Cavaliers marched out to the tune of 'Sir Henry Lingen's Fancy', which was to survive for the next two centuries as a country dance in South Herefordshire.

The capture of Goodrich was virtually the end of Birch's career.

The Colonel John Birch monument in Weobley Church, Herefordshire. (*Hereford and Worcester Libraries*)

On 9 December he entered the House of Commons and signed the Covenant as one of the members for the borough of Leominster.

Birch took advantage of his governorship of Hereford to speculate in church lands. He even purchased the Bishop's Palace!

A victim of Pride's Purge, Birch was actually seen riding with King Charles II at Worcester on the day before the battle! (1651). His opposition to Cromwell earned him imprisonment in Hereford Gaol from March to November 1655. Re-elected to Parliament in March 1656, he found himself excluded as one of the eighty who signed a protest. Re-elected in 1659 he played a prominent part in the Restoration, and was one of the new Council of State with Monck at its head.

King Charles evidently had a good idea of his loyalty and ability, and appointed him Auditor of the Excise for life, a reward which Birch repaid with twenty years' loyal service. This was, perhaps, some compensation for the loss of his church lands, whose purchase was nullified at the Restoration.

After the Great Fire, Birch produced a shrewd and practical

plan for the rebuilding of London.

In Parliament Birch proved an effective orator. Burnet wrote: 'He was the roughest and boldest speaker in the house, and talked in the language and phrases of a carrier, but with a beauty and eloquence that was always acceptable. I heard Coventry say he was the best speaker to carry a popular assembly before him that he had ever known.'

Colonel Francis Thornhagh (k. 1648). Sir Francis Thornhagh raised a regiment of horse in Nottinghamshire and appointed his eldest son, Francis, lieutenant-colonel (1642). Francis, like John Hutchinson, had been trained in arms by an old Low Country soldier, whilst still a schoolboy. Mrs Hutchinson tells us that:

> Francis Thornhagh, was a man of a most upright faithful heart to God and his people, and to his country's true interest, comprehended in the parliament's cause; a man of greater valour or more noble daring, fought not for them, nor indeed ever drew sword in any cause; he was of a most excellent good nature to all men, and zealous for his friend; he wanted counsel and deliberation, and was sometimes too facile to flatterers, but had judgment enough to discern his errors when they were represented to him, and worth enough not to persist in an injurious mistake because he had once entertained it.

Thornhagh was in the fight at Gainsborough (28 July 1643), when Lieutenant-General Charles Cavendish was killed, and in the subsequent defence of the town.

> Colonel Thornhagh, who had fought very gallantly, was taken prisoner, and after he was stripped of his arms and coat, a major of the enemy's, who the colonel had slightly wounded in the fervour of the fight, came and basely wounded the colonel, being disarmed, so that he left him for dead. But by the good providence of God, that wound, by which the enemy intended to give him death, gave him liberty; for coming to himself after his hurt, he crept into one of his own tenants' houses, and there had his wounds bound up and found means to get to Lincoln, . . .

When Prince Rupert relieved Newark (21 March 1644) Colonel

Thornhagh and Major Edward Rossiter gave the Cavaliers 'a very brave charge, routed those whom they first encountered, and took prisoners Major-general Charles Gerrard and others, and had they been seconded by the rest of the horse, had utterly defeated the prince's army; . . .'. However, the Lincolnshire horse fled before they ever charged, leaving Thornhagh engaged with the Prince's whole body'. . . they say he charged the prince himself, and . . . passed very gallantly through the whole army, with a great deal of honour, and two desperate wounds, one in the arm, the other in the belly . . .'. Thornhagh was not altogether unlucky, for though the rest were compelled to surrender, he was sent back to Nottingham in a wagon, and so was nursed back to health by his friends.

Thornhagh was an active and daring commander. The *London Post* of 16 December 1644 records that 'Colonel Thorney [*sic*] gave a great blow to a party of Sir John Girlington's horse at Muskham Bridge' . . . and no doubt this is an echo of but one of his many patrols and raids. A letter describing Rowton Moor, published in *Perfect Occurrences* for 9 October 1645, shows how Francis Thornhagh used to take his men into action:

> Sir, – In pursuit of the king so far I pursued, that retreat I could not, fight I must; commending myself and soldiers to God's protection, I resolved to charge them with my regiment. The enemy came down to us, and in a career charged; we stood and moved not till they had fired, which made Gerrard swear (God damn him), 'The rogues will not stir.' Upon those words we clapped spurs to our horses, and gave him such a charge as I daresay was the accomplishment of the victory, for we routed him and pursued him, and made him fly to Holt Castle, over a river in the night, with six men of a thousand which before were with him. – Francis Thornhagh, September 30.

Thornhagh played an active part in the Second Civil War of 1648.

> At this time Colonel Thornhagh marched with Cromwell, and at his parting with Colonel Hutchinson, took such a kind leave of him, with such dear expressions of love, such brotherly embraces, and such regret for any rash jealousies he had been wrought into, that it took great impression in the

The soldiers

A Royalist commission, 1642. Roger Whitley is appointed captain of a troop of horses in the regiment of Colonel Charles Gerard.

colonel's kind heart, and might have been a presage to him that they should meet no more, when they parted with such extraordinary melting love; but that Colonel Hutchinson's cheerful and constant spirit never anticipated any evil with fear. His prudence wanted not foresight that it might come, yet his faith and courage entertained his hope, that God would either prevent, or help him to bear it.

Thornhagh met his end at the battle of Preston.

Being at the beginning of the charge on a horse as courageous as became such a master, he made such furious speed to set upon a company of Scotch lancers, that he was singly engaged and mortally wounded, before it was possible for his regiment, though as brave as ever drew sword, and too

33

affectionate to their colonel, to be slack in following him, to come time enough to break the fury of that body, which shamed not to unite all their force against one man: who yet fell not among them, but being faint and all covered with blood, of his enemies as well as his own, was carried off by some of his own men, while the rest, enraged for the loss of their dear colonel, fought not that day like men of human race; but deaf to the cries of every coward that asked mercy, they killed all, and would not a captive should live to see their colonel die; but said the whole kingdom of Scotland was too mean a sacrifice for that brave man. His soul was hovering to take her flight out of his body, but that an eager desire to know the success of that battle kept it within till the end of the day, when the news being brought him, he cleared his dying countenance, and said, 'I now rejoice to die, since God hath let me see the overthrow of this perfidious enemy; I could not lose my life in a better cause, and I have the favour from God to see my blood avenged.'

Ludlow tells us that Thornhagh, when he knew he was mortally wounded, told his men 'to open to the right and left, that he might have the satisfaction to see them run before he died'.

Major Christopher Bethell (k. 1645).   Bethell first appears as the commander of the twelfth troop in Cromwell's famous double regiment. When the New Model was formed he became major of Colonel Edward Whalley's Regiment, one of the two formed out of the old Ironsides.

Early in the 1645 campaign he was taken prisoner 'engaging too far' in the skirmish with Goring's Horse at Radcot Bridge, but he was exchanged in time to fight at Naseby, where he routed one of Langdale's 'divisions' of horse, driving it back to Prince Rupert's Regiment, which was part of their reserve of foot.

Bethell particularly distinguished himself at Langport for with his troop he drove the Royalist foot from the ford of the Wagg Rhyne, and, went on to attack superior numbers of Cavaliers on the hill beyond. These, with the support of Major Desborow and some musketeers, he routed, at odds of at least two to one. Bethell was slightly wounded on this occasion. A month later he received his death wound at Bristol. 'I wish', wrote Hugh Peters the chaplain, 'he may not go unlamented to his grave, who was so full of God, and the fairest flower of the city[5] amongst us; he

lived without pride, and died full of faith.' In Sprigg's *Anglia
Rediviva* there is a truly awful eulogistic poem, attributed to
Peters, and entitled 'The Army's Tears over Major Bethell'.

Bethell was an honest man, and a good fighting soldier of the
old Ironside breed. His brief military career must have been
typical of scores who fought for the cause of the Parliament.

Sergeant Nehemiah Wharton (d. 1642?). During the First Civil
War it was by no means every NCO that could read and write. It
may be that those Parliamentarian regiments which recruited in
London were exceptional in this respect. There is an excellent
account of the relief of Gloucester and First Newbury by Sergeant
Henry Foster of the Red Regiment of the London Trained Bands.[6]
Even more interesting are the letters of Sergeant Nehemiah
Wharton of Colonel Denzil Holles' Regiment relating his
adventures in the Edgehill campaign.[7]

Wharton's correspondent was his master, one Willingham,
and before he joined the army he was evidently an apprentice,
perhaps one of those who rioted about the Palace of Whitehall at
Christmas 1641, and felt, some of them, the sharpness of
Lunsford's sword, and those of his unemployed officers.
Certainly Wharton had no liking for professional soldiers. To him
Colonel Thomas Ballard and Lieutenant-Colonel Henry Billingsley were profane wretches. Of the latter, whose disciplinary
ideas were unpopular, Wharton wrote as 'a Godamme blade, and
doubtlesse hatche in hell, and we all desire that ether the
Parliament would depose him, or God convert him, or the Devill
fetch him away quick' (10 August). When Billingsley ordered two
captains to march out of Aylesbury, Wharton describes it as an
'ungrounded whimsey'.

The discipline of Essex's army of 1642 was strange indeed.
Many had enlisted from base motives, others thought of the
campaign as a country holiday from their narrow city streets.
There was much ill feeling between horse and foot, and on 4
September 'Colonel Foynes' Troop[8] robbed the sergeant of goods
worth £3. Wharton threatened to order his musketeers to open
fire on them.

Though the soldiers themselves did not care for discipline,
at Coventry on 27 August Wharton records with some
satisfaction the fate of a harlot, who had followed the army
from London. 'The soldiers took her and led her about the
city, set her in the pillory and afterwards in the cage. Then

they ducked her in a river, and at last they banished her.'

The army did little training. Wharton makes no mention of any before 17 September. The men much preferred breaking up churches, tormenting the clergy and slaughtering deer. They were not slow to plunder a papist or a malignant. Above all they loved a sermon from worthy Mr Obadiah Sedgewick or another.

The weather in the England of 1642 was just as odd as it is today and Wharton actually records that near Hereford on 30 September a soldier died 'by reason of the raine and snow, and extremitie of cold'.

Wharton has left a number of sidelights on the rather dreadful Roundhead Army of 1642. One of the more pleasant is his mention (30 August) of what was doubtless an ancient and honourable custom. 'Tuesday morning we officers wet our halberts [the sergeants' weapon] with a barrel of strong beere, called ould Hum, which we gave our soldiers.'

Wharton's series of letters end shortly before Edgehill. Would that we had so lively an observer's account of that famous fight. But it seems likely that this intelligent Puritan soldier went down when Rupert's Horse broke through the ranks of Holles' Regiment.

Notes

1. The Western Cavaliers under Sir John Stawell had won a decided victory at Marshall's Elm, Somerset in August.
2. A sixteenth-century mine may still be seen at St Andrews in Scotland.
3. From the regiment of foot commanded by Sir Charles Vavasour and, after his death (Sir) Matthew Appleyard.
4. Not *John* as in the monument which may be seen in the church.
5. Presumably he was a Londoner.
6. *True and Exact Relation*. John Washbourne. *Bibliotheca Gloucestrensis*, 2 vols, Gloucester (1823).
7. Wharton, 'Letters'.
8. Nathaniel Fiennes.

CHAPTER 3

Oxford in the Civil Wars

Tis probable this venerable doctor [Ralph Kettell] might
have lived some years longer, and finished his century, had
not those civil wars come on; which much grieved him, that
was wont to be absolute in the college, to be affronted and
disrespected by rude soldiers.

John Aubrey

One afternoon in 1935, whilst an undergraduate of Trinity
College, I wandered into the showrooms of the Clarendon Press
in the High. There my eye lit upon a pamphlet entitled 'The Siege
of Oxford'. I cannot pretend that at the age of twenty I was well
versed in the history of our Civil Wars, though I was, I suppose,
already aware that the Roundheads were *Right but Repulsive,*
while the Cavaliers were *Wrong but Romantic.* Somehow the little
book stirred in me thoughts of Prince Rupert riding out to Glory
and Honour afar, and I purchased it – I think for sixpence. That
evening I lay in my bath and read it. Trinity had no baths before
the First World War, I am told; but then some soldiers were
quartered there who could not stomach the Spartan ways of men,
who were after all, only up for eight weeks. Baths, deep and
comfortable, with a very efficient water supply were installed –
presumably by the War Office – and they were excellent places for
light reading. But the pamphlet was brief, and proved to be but a
supplement. I was compelled to return next day to the OUP and
purchase the book itself: *The Siege of Oxford* by F. J. Varley. I can
only honour an author, who had such a great effect on my life; but
it must be said that he was no great hand at reading seventeenth
century writing. At one point he manages to turn Colonel
Pinchbeck into Colonel Lunsford. Not bad. But that is a rather
minor black. My main criticism was – and is – that he provided no
map.

Civil War England

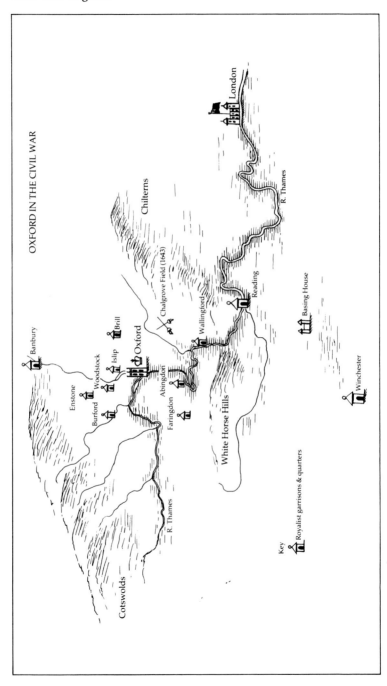

OXFORD IN THE CIVIL WAR

London

R. Thames

Chilterns

Chalgrove Field (1643)

Banbury

Brill

Woodstock

Islip

Oxford

Enstone

Burford

Abingdon

Faringdon

Wallingford

Reading

Basing House

Winchester

White Horse Hills

R. Thames

Cotswolds

Key

Royalist garrisons & quarters

By this time I was hooked on the Civil War, so I decided to make my own. I purchased Ordnance Survey maps of every sort and set to to mark in every sort of building that I conceived had been there in 1642. It was fascinating. I read every college history I could lay my hands on. But mostly I trudged – as I hope you will – I trudged every street, marked every surviving tower of the mediaeval walls, the mounds where Naomi Mitchison played in her youth, the cobbled Merton Street, the ancient houses in St Aldates, and on the way I was compelled to see whether, in my judgement, The Bear was the sort of place that was already selling ale when Sir Arthur Aston, testy and imperious, governed that loyal city. It was great fun, and I was, I think, pretty bad at it. And an evening came, when Paul Something-or-other, whose surname does not really escape me, planted a wet pint pot on the corner of my map and rather destroyed its pristine beauty. What the hell? By that time it was too late. My interest in that long-forgotten war had grown far beyond the limits of the Royalist capital. On a prowl round Thornton's I had found Warburton's *Prince Rupert and the Cavaliers* (3 vols. 18s.). On a lucky day in the North Room of the College Library I had found Symonds' *Diary* (Camden Society, 1859), and what a regale that is to one who would know the old Cavalier Army. Then there was a lucky day when I went to the study/library of the Rev. J. R. H. Weaver for a tutorial and he was not there. Prowling his shelves I came upon Hopton's *Bellum Civile*. An hour later Weaver returned and (perhaps a trifle ashamed) lent me the book. Hopton was not only a first-rate general, but a master of Clarendonian prose. I honour Weaver greatly – he was afterwards President and entertained me nobly when I returned to Trinity after the Second World War. But he certainly did me a good turn by his tardiness that day.

Another great piece of luck was the discovery, of Sir Bernard de Gomme's map of Oxford, described long since in *Oxoniensia*. In my ignorance I had supposed that the Royalist defences had followed the line of the mediaeval walls. No such thing. The line was constructed, at great expense, outside the then built-up area. The formidable earthworks, which cost £30,000 when Aston was Governor, ran just south of the Parks, and included Holywell Church in a kind of bastion. By the middle of the last century they had more or less disappeared. Indeed, when the University Museum was built they had to dig the foundations a great deal deeper than expected, because they crossed the old Cavalier

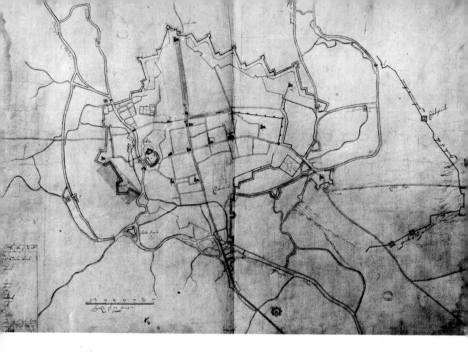

Oxford beseiged. A contemporary plan showing the Royalist's defences by Sir Bernard de Gomme (1620–85). (*The Curators of the Bodleian Library, Oxford*)

ditch and line. Across the road the chapel of Keble College early developed a great crack, owing to subsidence organized 200 years earlier by Royalist engineers.

The main defences were on the north side, for Oxford is otherwise well defended by water obstacles, but there were other works including a bridgehead east of Magdalen Bridge.

Oxford made a good capital for the Royalists. Strategically it is the centre of the South Midlands. Its ring of satellite fortresses, of which the chief were Banbury, Wallingford, Abingdon and Faringdon, secured a good tract of farming country, which helped to support the garrison. The buildings of the University provided accommodation for the King and his court at Christ Church, and for the Queen at Merton, as well as a magazine for the Board of Ordnance in the little quadrangle of New College and a gun park in Magdalen Grove.

The castle served as a prison – a singularly uncomfortable one it seems. The Roundhead, Edmund Ludlow, who matriculated at Trinity College in 1634 returned to Oxford as a prisoner of war

Overleaf: Jan Wyck's painting of the Siege of Oxford, showing clearly the city's extensive defences. (*Reproduced by kind permission of Lord Dartmouth*)

after his determined defence of Wardour Castle wrote:

> In the castle of Oxford I met with Mr. Balsum, and other
> friends, who had been with me in Warder-castle, and many
> more who were detained there for their affection to the
> parliament, amongst whom were colonel Shilborn of
> Buckinghamshire, and colonel Henly of Dorsetshire, captain
> Haley of Glocestershire, and captain [Jeconiah] Abercromy a
> Scots-man. I had a friend in the town who furnished me with
> what I wanted: those who had not any such means of relief,
> were supplied from London by a collection of the sum of
> three hundred pounds, made for them by some citizens, who
> conveyed [it] down to them. Neither was Oxford itself
> destitute of some who contributed to their relief; one Dr.
> Hobbs in particular, who preached then at Carfax, an honest
> man of the episcopal party, usually putting them in mind of it
> after his sermon.

The Oxford Parliament, which the king, somewhat tactlessly,
described as 'our mongrel Parliament here', met in Christ Church
Hall on 22 January 1644. Forty-four lords and 118 members of the
Commons were present, and they contributed enough money to
see 'the Oxford Army' through its successful campaign of 1644,
enabling Charles to defeat Waller at Cropredy Bridge and cut off
Essex at Lostwithiel.

The buildings of the University were converted into magazines
for corn, tailors' shops and a variety of other military uses. The
schools being occupied, lectures and examinations were held in
the North Chapel of St Mary's Church.

It was all very exciting – not to say demoralizing – for the
students. Anthony Wood, the antiquary, tells us they were
'much debauched and became idle by their bearing arms, and
keeping company with rude soldiers'. Undergraduates, then and
later, were not altogether against experiments in debauchery.
Many an idle hour was spent in gaming, drinking and awful
singing at the Holly Bush Inn or the Angel near Rewley.

The three sieges of Oxford were of a somewhat desultory
character. It is true that Prince Rupert received his only wound of
the war whilst skirmishing during the last siege. The
Roundheads proved indifferent gunners. Their first shot, fired
on 13 May 1646 from their great work on Headington Hill, fell
harmlessly in Christ Church Meadow.

St Mary's Church, Oxford. On 20 September 1642 a Roundhead trooper discharged a brace of bullets at the stone image of Our Lady over the church porch, and struck off her head, and the head of her child which she held in her right arm. (*A. F. Kersting*)

The crowded streets of the old city witnessed some strange scenes in those days. The undisciplined Roundhead soldiers of 1642, bluecoats and russet coats, brawling in the High Street at Carfax and about the Star (30 September), using their newly issued swords to cut off each others' thumbs. The luckless Virgin over the door of St Mary's Church found herself the target of a Roundhead carbine one day in 1642. There was a wooden horse over against the Guildhall and a gibbet at Carfax conduit.

A main guard was kept at Carfax. Tom Quad saw Rupert, poleaxe in hand, come forth in a rage to part two officers who having quarrelled over a horse, had lugged out their swords. And again one evening some gentleman, who had taken against the detested Catholic Governor, stuck him in the side with his rapier. Thenceforth Sir Arthur Aston was escorted by halberdiers dressed in long red cassocks.

Upon the lighter side we find Mrs Fanshawe and Mrs Thynne, dressed like angels, calling on the formidable old President, Ralph Kettell (1563–1643), of Trinity in order to tease him. John Aubrey, who went up to Oxford in 1643, tells us this Elizabethan relic 'had a terrible gigantic aspect with his sharp grey eyes . . . he had a very venerable presence, and was an excellent governor'. Though charitable, he believed in keeping down youthful enthusiasm [*juvenilis impetuus*], and was 'a right Church of England man'. Aubrey explains:

> Our grove was the Daphne for the ladies and their gallants to walk in, and many times my Lady Isabella Thynne would

New College, Oxford. The cloister where the Royalist artillery had its magazine, 1642–46. (*National Monuments Record Crown Copyright reserved*)

make her entry with a thearbo or lute played before her. I have heard her play on it in the grove myself, which she did rarely; for which Mr Edmund Waller has in his *Poems* for ever made her famous. . . . She was most beautiful, most humble, charitable, etc but she could not subdue one thing. I remember one time this lady and fine Mrs [Richard] Fanshawe (her great and intimate friend, who lay at our college) would have a frolic to make a visit to the president. The old doctor quickly perceived that they came to abuse him; he addressed his discourse to Mrs Fanshawe, saying 'Madam, your husband and father I bred up here, and I knew your grandfather; I know you to be a gentlewoman, I will not say you are a whore; but get you gone for a very woman.' The dissoluteness of the times . . . grieving the good old doctor, his days were shortened and [he] died in 1643, and was buried at Garsington.

What with officers and soldiers quartered in every street; a fire that destroyed much of the Cornmarket, from North Gate (Bocardo) to Carfax (6 October 1644) and three sieges, it was a difficult time, however exciting, what with musters of the garrison in New Parks and so on. Mrs Fanshawe tells us what it was like for the families of the Cavaliers:

> . . . My father commanded my sister and myself to come to him to Oxford where the Court then was, but we, that had till that hour lived in great plenty and great order, found ourselves like fishes out of the water, and the scene was so changed, that we knew not at all how to act any part but obedience, for, from as good a house as any gentleman of England had, we came to a baker's house in an obscure street, and from rooms well furnished, to lie in a very bad bed in a garret, to one dish of meat, and that not the best ordered, no money, for we were as poor as Job, nor clothes more than a man or two brought in their cloak bags: we had the perpetual discourse of losing and gaining towns and men; at the windows the sad spectacle of war, sometimes plague, sometimes sicknesses of other kind, by reason of so many

people being packed together, as, I believe, there never was
before of that quality; always in want, yet I must needs say
that most bore it with a martyr-like cheerfulness. For my own
part, I began to think we should all, like Abraham, live in
tents all the days of our lives. . . .

Oxford has been called the home of lost causes. It was not
perhaps a very comfortable one for the Cavaliers, being rather too
much in the front line to be really secure. Nevertheless, it was
perhaps the most important result of the Edgehill campaign that
the city fell into the King's hands and furnished him with an
adequate capital for the next four years.

Coins minted in Oxford during the Civil Wars. (Top left) Charles I; gold unite,
1642. (Top middle) Charles I; gold unite, 1644. (Top right) Charles I; gold
half-unite, 1643. (Bottom) Charles I; pound, 1643. (*The Curators of the Ashmolean
Museum, Oxford*)

CHAPTER 4

Arms and armour

My Lord Belasyse 'found himself engaged in the midst of Sir
Thomas Fairfax' troops, who killed his horse under him and
discharged some pistols and blows with swords at him: so as
he had certainly beene slain but for the goodness of his arms,
and thereby received but two wounds; one in his arm, the
other in his head; both with swords: so as (tho' he asked it
not), yet they gave him quarter, and carried him to the Lord
Fairfax, their General and my Lord's near kinsman, who
treated him civilly and sent his chirurgeon to dress his
wounds, . . . '.

Joshua Moone, writing of the fight at Selby, 11 April 1644.

The armies of the Civil Wars consisted of a rudimentary staff; of
horse, dragoons and foot and a train of artillery. The horse and
foot were organized in regiments and sometimes in brigades, or
tertias. Dragoons sometimes formed separate regiments, and
sometimes companies, or troops, in the regiments of horse. An
army seldom numbered more than 15,000 men, sometimes far
less, and from 12 to 20 guns of various sizes was considered a
sufficient train for a marching army.

In theory a regiment of horse or foot numbered 500 or 1,200
men respectively, but in practice such numbers were seldom
attained. One of the greatest mistakes made by the Royalists was
to commission far too many regiments. Nor can the Roundheads
be held altogether guiltless of this administrative error. Certainly
they attempted to hold a vast number of garrisons, many of them
of little strategic value. In this respect both sides laid themselves
open to criticism. Naturally, there was no continuous front line in
those days – nothing like the trench system that stretched from
Switzerland to the sea in the First World War, or the *ne plus ultra*

lines of Marlborough's day. Roundhead and Cavalier tried to secure his own territory with garrisons, whose range was not so much that of their few cannon, but of their marauding troop of horse.

Uniform was in its infancy in 1642. Soldiers often wore their civilian costume. Nevertheless, there were general issues of clothing, equipment, armour and weapons, and these tended to give a regiment an air of uniformity. Even so, martinets of 100 years later would, no doubt, have been shocked to their narrow souls by the sad state of military millinery at Cheriton or Cropredy. Cumberland and Hawley would have been grieved indeed at the lack of powder and pomatum; of facings and gaiters, and it is true that the uniforms of Dettingen and Brandywine Creek were much prettier and better cut than those of Naseby. Our Civil War ancestors, like King Henry V's followers, were 'but warriors for the working day'; and to see how soldierlike some of them looked you need but visit the National Portrait Gallery and gaze upon the portrait of the fierce-tempered Sir Charles Lucas; or Broughton Castle and admire Colonel Nathaniel Fiennes – though in truth he looks

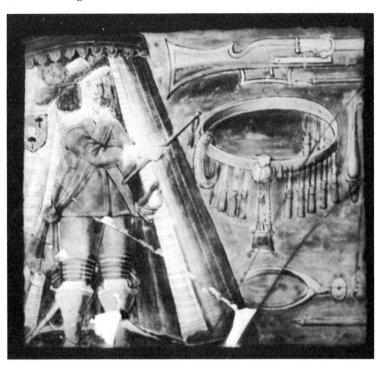

Farndon Church window showing soldiers of Colonel Sir Francis Gamul's Regiment of Foot. (Top left) the Colonel with a musket bandolier and bullet-mould; (Bottom left) from left to right, sergeant, ensign and fifer; (Above) Captain William Barnston of Churton, his partisan and gorget are, in effect, his badges of rank. (*Eileen Preston*)

more warlike than he proved. These two seem to me to be the very type of Cavalier and Roundhead. Both are shown as cavalrymen, though it is likely that general officers on either side accoutred themselves after much the same fashion.

The most practical way to study the weapons of the Civil War is to spend a day – or better two – in visiting the Armouries in the White Tower at HM Tower of London. Here you will find arms and armour of every kind for both horse and foot. Much of it you will observe dates from periods earlier than the Civil Wars, and has been converted to conform with changing fashion. A morion that had served against the Armada was by no means unserviceable in 1642. One hangs in Kendal Church, which belonged to a Cavalier, Captain Phillipson, alias 'Robin the

Devil', which is clearly of the 1588 pattern. One may suppose that in 1642 fresh supplies were hard to come by in the wilds of Westmorland.

With the exception of a buff-coat which belonged to the regicide Colonel Francis Hacker (d. 1660), the Civil War equipment in the Tower cannot be attributed to any particular persons. But at Littlecote House near Hungerford a fine family collection is preserved. This belonged to the Popham family, which produced two Roundhead colonels, Alexander (1605–69) and Edward (*c.* 1607–51), and a judge, whose elegant finger-stocks may still be seen: he evidently disliked his prisoners fidgeting about whilst he was talking to them. There is an equestrian portrait of Colonel Alexander in full armour, baton in hand and with an unusual hanger at his side. He rides a small, strong, wise-looking grey, speckled with spots the size of currants.

Fortunately, the house is open to the public and it is very well worth a visit. The collection of arms and armour includes several three-quarter suits such as Sir Arthur Hesilrige's famous 'Lobsters' wore not far away at Roundway Down above Devizes, when they were routed on 13 July 1643 and driven in dramatic fashion down the hill 'where never horse went down or up before' – a horrible fate.

Littlecote has more buff-coats than any other collection in the kingdom, and they are complete with the crossbelts for carbine and sword, such as the normal trooper carried, whichever side he was on. It is a nineteenth-century artist's convention that the Cavaliers wore plumed hats and cloaks, while the Puritans wore grimly blackened breastplates and lobster-tailed helmets. Doubtless the warriors of either side blackened their armour to keep off the rust – there was no Brasso in those days – and anyone, Roundhead or Cavalier, got hold of a helmet as soon as he could.

Many a museum up and down the country has its collection of weapons, but there can be few like that at Littlecote which was closely connected with one family. Even so, the collection at Farleigh Hungerford is worth a visit.

To find authentic Civil War cannon is not easy. There is a fine mortar at Hereford, which threw 'granadoes' into Goodrich Castle, near Ross, when Colonel Sir Henry Lingen held the place for the King (see p. 55). Two small guns of the period are on display in the Tower, and the great gun at Dover Castle, though

'Roaring Meg'. Probably the only surviving mortar of the Civil Wars. It was made in the Forest of Dean for Colonel John Birch, and was employed against Goodrich and Raglan Castles. It can now be seen at the Churchill Museum, Hereford. (*S. B. Webb*)

dating from the Tudor period, cannot be very unlike the 14-foot cannon, with the rose and crown engraved upon it, which was amongst the spoils when Hopton routed the Roundheads at Braddock Down (19 January 1643).

The aspect of a Royalist infantry unit is well shown in the almost contemporary church window at Farndon in Cheshire. These are the officers and men of Colonel Sir Francis Gamul's Regiment of Foot, part of the garrison of Chester. Though a few of the figures are taken from pictures of the *Gardes Françaises*, most seem to be original and they include small full-length portraits of Gamul himself, and officers from the local families of Barnston and Mainwaring. A sergeant, an ensign, a fifer and Captain William Barnston of Churton are shown, and all sorts of items of equipment, such as the mould for making musket bullets.

On a monument in the church at Patshull, Warwickshire,

Captain Richard Astley, Bt (1662), rides at the head of his troop of Cavaliers. The cinquefoil of Astley may be seen on his holster-caps, and his saddle-cloth, and on the standard of the troop as well as the trumpet banners. The two trumpeters, both of whom resemble those in contemporary Dutch paintings, wear beaver hats of the sort Ernest Crofts used to put on his Cavaliers, and hanging sleeves. This troop, which belonged to Lord Loughborough's command in the Midlands, was evidently light or medium cavalry. They are not wearing body armour, except for buff-coats and the occasional gorget. Astley died, aged sixty-three in 1688, and it may be that the monument was made a generation after the Civil Wars.

The Golden Cavalier, Captain Edward St John, who may be seen in the little church at Lydiard Tregoz near Swindon, is as much a cuirassier as any of Hesilrige's lobsters. Some Victorian had the odious idea of painting over the fading colours of the monument with gold, but could not altogether disguise the authentic heavy cavalryman of the day. Details such as the cord which held the spanner to wind up his wheel-lock pistols show that this is a real warrior and not just a piece of funerary armour.

The soldiers on either side wore expensive sashes – even the ordinary ones cost about 10s. each. At first, at any rate in theory,

Parliamentarian cavalry standards. Twistleton was colonel from 1647–59, but Nelthorpe and Pearte were captains in the regiment as early as 1645, and probably had these colours at Naseby. (*Dr William's Library*)

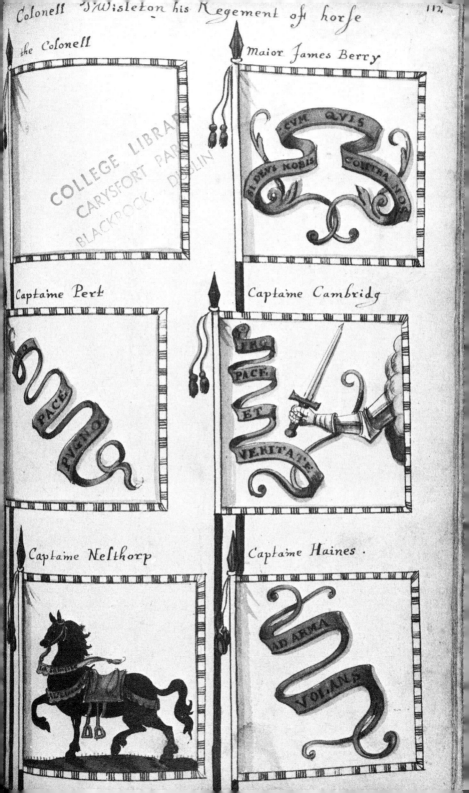

the Colonell

Maior James Berry

SI CVM QVIS
SI DEVS NOBIS CONTRA NOS

Captaine Pert

Captaine Cambridg

PACE PIGNO

IAC PACE ET VERITATE

Captaine Nelthorp

Captaine Haines

AD ARMA VOLANS

the Royalists wore scarves of rose-pink and the Roundheads favoured the orange/tawny colours of their captain-general, 'Old Robin', the Earl of Essex (1591–1646).

A word on colours.

Each troop and company had a standard, a guidon (dragoons) or a colour. Thus there were ten in an infantry regiment. It seems an awful lot of potential trophies, but in those days when the soldiery were unlettered, they needed something they could recognize to rally on. The infantry system was simple enough. The colonel tended, if he was armigerous – and for the most part the colonels of either side were – to choose the field of his coat of arms for his colours. The colonel's was absolutely plain; the lieutenant-colonel's had a small St George's cross in the upper canton; the major added a flame emerging from this canton. The captain's colours were often differenced by some charge taken from the colonel's arms – the dog of Talbot, the lions of Saye and Sele and so on.

Cavalry standards tended to display political slogans, or pious exhortations. Few, if any, colours seem to have survived from those distant days. There are said to be two in the church at Bromsberrow, measuring 2 feet by 2 feet.

The cavalry of the Civil Wars were, in general, not unlike the cuirassiers of Napoleon's day. They would have felt pretty much at home on the field of Waterloo. The horses they sought, one supposes, were much the same as those ridden by the heavy cavalry of Wellington's day. The cobs and lighter horses were assigned to the dragoons, who were trained to fight on foot.

The infantry of the Civil Wars period had vanished by the time of Blenheim. Under Marlborough every musketeer was his own pikeman. The invention of the bayonet, and of the iron ramrod transformed the infantry. In the days of the Civil Wars an infantry regiment was clumsy indeed. A hedgehog of pikemen was flanked by two bodies of musketeers, whose rate of fire was painfully slow. Even so, good, resolute, steady foot could keep out horse upon occasion.

The artillery, too, had many drawbacks. Batteries were formed for a siege, but in battle the guns were usually worked in pairs.

A Harquebusier, the cavalryman of the Civil Wars, with his triple-barred helmet, left-hand guard, buff coat and carbine. Royalists as well as Roundheads dressed like this, and both wore sashes or scarves to show which side they were on. (*Crown Copyright – reproduced with the permission of the Controller of Her Majesty's Stationery Office*)

They were dragged into position by horses and left. It was seldom if ever that they could be moved once a battle had begun. Planks had to be laid under the wheels, so that the guns could run back smoothly: otherwise they would gradually dash their carriages to pieces as they recoiled. The horses were harnessed tandem, and so even a large team wasted a lot of effort. It was not for another century at least that artillery horses were harnessed in pairs.

The rate of fire was slow, for the loading drill was complicated, and the provision of ammunition was but small; about fifty rounds per gun, with perhaps half a dozen rounds of case-shot, would be normal.

The horse-drawn armies of the Civil Wars moved slowly along the broad rutted roads of the period, making 15 miles a day if they were lucky, and living, like locusts, off a land, where as yet barbed wire was unknown, and enclosures were comparatively rare. It may be asserted that forest and downland met the eye far more commonly than now: swamps like Otmoor were as yet undrained. The weather, if anything, was even worse than it is today. Even so, for anyone with a taste for commando soldiering, it must have been a great life . . . at any rate a great deal better than Passchendaele or the jungles of Burma.

CHAPTER 5

The battles

O Lord! Thou knowest how busy I must be this day.
If I forget Thee, do not Thou forget me.
Sergeant-Major-General Sir Jacob Astley

> I was admitted into Prince Maurice's regiment, which was
> accounted the most active regiment in the army, and most
> commonly placed in the out quarters; which gave me more
> proficiency as a soldier, in half a year's time, than generally in
> the Low Countries in 4 or 5 years; for there did hardly one
> week pass in the summer half year, in which there was not a
> battle or skirmish fought, or beating up quarters; which
> indeed lasted the whole year, insomuch as for three weeks at
> most, I commanded the forlorn-hope thrice.
> Captain Richard Atkyns

Richard Atkyns first saw action at Little Dean on 11 April 1643.
After the taking of Bristol (26 July) he came to the remarkable
conclusion that the King's crown was settled upon his head
again, and desired leave to return to his private condition. And so
he only had about four months' active service. Even so his
statement that there was a great deal more fighting in our Civil
Wars than in the Low Country wars of the same period, cannot be
parried. In those days when it was customary to go into winter
quarters our ancestors, both Cavalier and Roundhead, carried
out countless operations at that season. Indeed, there was so
much fighting that it is not always easy to discern any underlying
strategic pattern. Nor is it simple to draw a line between
skirmishes and combats, actions and battles. Roundway Down,
for example, was obviously a battle, yet the Royalist Army
comprised no more than 1,800 horse with a handful of gunners.
The fact is that armies were often small. A body of 5,000–7,000, a

mere brigade group we should think it today, was considered a handsome marching army: the Cornish Army that fought Stratton is a good example.

King Charles, at the head of his main army, fought two major battles, Second Newbury and Naseby, with less than 10,000 men present. At Marston Moor, the biggest battle of the war, and perhaps the biggest ever fought on English soil,[1] not more than 50,000 men took part, and that number was achieved only because there were five armies present. The population of the country was probably in the region of 5 million, and it is perhaps strange that, with great issues at stake, such comparatively small bodies of men should have been left to decide the issue. But there were, of course, many men in arms, who never saw a pitched battle, and smelt powder but seldom. They formed the garrisons of those scores of fortresses with which each side endeavoured to hold down the country. Some of these places were very small, and could be held with but few men. Donnington Castle, watching the River Kennet at Newbury, is an example – its earthworks can still be traced. Its Cavalier garrison consisted of 200 foot, 25 horse and 4 guns, and was evidently self-supporting. How so? Quite simple. When not actually beleaguered the soldiers ranged about the country helping themselves to anything they needed: food, drink, bedding, anything.

A Royalist colonel, Sir William Savile, wrote on 21 June 1643 to his major, Thomas Beaumont, the Governor of Sheffield Castle: '. . . bee sure you want not any mony nether for your selfe nor your frends, soe long as any Roundhead hath either fingers or toas left, within tenn myles of the Castle'. The range of a garrison was not the range of its guns – say 800 yards – but the range of its troop of horse, which could move out under cover of darkness; make its raid at dawn and be home before the hue and cry could be raised. Raiding – beating up of quarters – was a very popular form of military operation during the Civil Wars. You cannot go 5 miles in the Midlands without stumbling upon the scene of one of those long-forgotten fights. Drive from Chipping Norton to Stow-on-the-Wold and after a time you will see on your left the

Donnington Castle. Traces of the Civil War earthworks can be seen outside the old foundations, especially to the right of the picture. Colonel Sir John Boys, with some 200 Royalist soldiers, held the castle from 1642 to 1646. One may imagine him observing the second battle of Newbury from the towers of the gatehouse. (*Aerofilms Limited*)

sign to Oddington. It is a sleepy little place in a pleasant country. Who would think that such an innocent place had ever been the scene of a violent combat? Yet there was a stiff bout there on Friday, 23 June 1643, when Colonel Edward Massey, ranging far from his garrison at Gloucester, clashed with Charles Gerard's men. *Mercurius Aulicus*, the Oxford weekly, 'Communicating the Intelligence and affaires of the Court, to the rest of the KINGDOME' reports this action (p. 329):

> Newes came this day that certaine of the *Rebels* in *Glocestershire* (conducted by Colonel *Stevens* of *Effington*) had fallen the night before on Colonel *Charles Gerrards* quarters at Odington not farre from *Stowe*: and having surprized the said Colonels brother Captaine *Gerard* with some of his inferiour Officers (as if they had beene theeves not soldiers) they ran away with their booty. News whereof was brought to some of their neighbours quarters, who presently pursued after them so feircely, that they redeemed all the prisoners, killed two Captaines, and tooke Colonel *Stevens* himselfe, with some other men of note and quality, and so returned againe to their owne in safety, sending their Prisoners towards *Oxford*, in this pursuit Sergeant Major *Francis Ruce* (who behaved himselfe very bravely) received a wound, but nothing dangerous.

In its next issue *Mercurius* followed up the story, under 26 June:

> This day we had intelligence, that Lieutenant *Jay* (Lieutenant to Captain *Tyrrell*) is dead of that wound he received on Friday last in the defeat given to the *Gloucester* Rebels by some Troopes commanded by Lieutenant Colonell *David Walter*, Serjeant Major *Dubbleday*, Serjeant Major *Ruse*, Captain *Russell*, Captain *Leigh*, and others, who all carried themselves as bravely as men could do, especially this Lieutenant *Jay* who led on the *Forlorne Hope* exceeding valiantly, killing with his own hand the Captain that led on the Rebels Forces. In this service was done so good execution that yester morning 200 Rebels came with divers Carts to fetch away their wounded and dead men, with which they filled their Carts, besides what the Countrey had buried. Of the Kings partie there were onely three slain, and four or five wounded (besides Major *Ruse*, who being shot upon his money-pocket did him little hurt) Captain *Leigh* and Master

Robert Masters had two slight hurts, the Lieutenant Colonels Corporall was shot through both his cheekes, and one of Captain *Russels* Troopers was somewhat cut, which was all the hurt those Rebels then did us.

Master Robert Masters, a Gloucestershire man, figures in the 1663 list of indigent officers. He had been cornet to Major-General David Walters under Lord Gerard.

Oddington was hardly a battle, but even raids and *chevauchées* of that sort have their effect if skilfully handled, and attended with little loss.

Even so it is the big battles that most capture our imagination, partly because of their more clearly decisive nature, and partly because the commanders on either side tended to be the real diehards in the struggle between King and Parliament.

The first of the big battles was Edgehill, fought between Kineton and Banbury on land much of which is now occupied by the Central Ammunition Depot, Kineton, and which the public may not readily visit. That was not so on my first visit, forty-four years ago, when I bicycled there from Oxford with the late F. P. Powell (Monmouth and BNC). What energy! Unfortunately, in those days when one could so readily inspect the field very little was known about the way the battle was fought. Godfrey Davies, in an article in the *English Historical Review*, had endeavoured to piece together the Royalist order of battle, but it was still largely conjectural. After the war, however, the Rev. Percy Sumner, searching the Royal Library at Windsor for information upon uniforms, came across Sir Bernard de Gomme's plan, and brought it to my attention. Although he omits the dragoons and the cannon de Gomme gives us the line-up of the Royalist horse and foot, we owe him a great debt of gratitude. Even so one can only regret that another map, made in February 1643, has disappeared.

Sir William Dugdale, the Herald, tells us that

having taken notice of the most memorable passages in that Battell . . . in February next ensuing, being accompanied wth some Gentlemen of note, taking wth him a skylfull Surveyor [Mr Holsted], he rode . . . to the Feild where the Battell was fought; wch he exactly surveyed, noting where each Army was drawn up; how the Canon placed; and the graves where the slayn were buryed; . . .

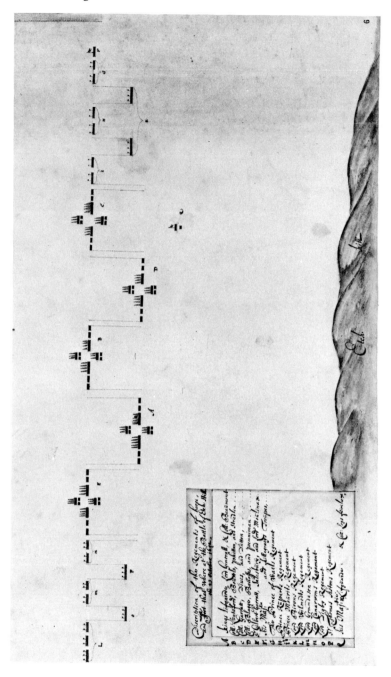

What became of the result of all this labour? Nobody seems to know. . . .

The Parliamentarians with far greater financial resources at their disposal, had raised their army some time before the king was ready to take the field. The Earl of Essex, no great strategist, had advanced slowly to Worcester. Perhaps he thought the King, who was at Shrewsbury, intended to push down the Severn Valley and take Bristol. In fact the King decided – a far more correct strategy – to attempt to capture London. On 12 October, rather late in the campaigning season, he began his advance, moving slowly through the Midlands.

At this early stage neither side was much good at reconnaissance, and when on 22 October their quartermasters, looking for billets, clashed near Kineton, both were considerably surprised.

Next morning early the Royalists concentrated on the top of Edge Hill, planting the great Banner Royal somewhere near the public house, the Castle, whose tower overlooks the Vale of the Red Horse. Essex, who had spent several of his regiments in garrisoning towns – Gloucester, Hereford, Coventry and so on – drew out his army south of Kineton in full view of the Cavaliers. It soon became evident that he had no intention of storming the steep down which is Edge Hill. And so the Royalists, very obligingly, marched down into the valley and drew up near Radway.

They set to partners in a fairly conventional fashion, but the arrangements made by the generals on either side are open to serious criticism. The Royalists kept no proper reserve, and arrayed their infantry in an order too complicated for semi-trained troops: the Swedish Brigade. However, they had five brigades of foot, and a pentagonal tactical organization is perhaps the most flexible that can be devised. Essex had only three brigades of foot, and instead of dividing his horse more or less equally between each wing, decided to place two regiments, his best ones as it turned out, behind and in support of one of the infantry brigades.

The relative strength of each side was probably something like this:

Sir Bernard de Gomme's plan of the Royalist army at the battle of Edge Hill, 23 October 1642. (*Reproduced by gracious permission of Her Majesty the Queen*)

	King	Essex
Horse	2,800	2,150
Dragoons	1,000	720
Foot	10,500	12,000
Guns	20	30–37
	14,300	14,870

The battle that followed was far from complicated. After the usual giving out of orders and exhortations there was a preliminary bombardment, which may have done a bit of harm to the nerves of troops unaccustomed to such unpleasant attentions, but probably scored very few direct hits. Then the Royalists advanced, and in the nature of things the cavalry got there first, but not before the dragoons had cleared the flanks of Roundhead dragoons and musketeers. So little resistance did the Roundhead cavalry make that it might have been possible, one might think, for the second line of the Royalist cavalry on each wing to wheel inwards and assist their own infantry in their attack upon Essex's foot. It was not to be. Gentlemen, more accustomed to the chase than to the field of battle, set off in pursuit of their prey, as if a Parliamentarian was a buck or a fox. Rap one or two of them on his round head with sword or poleaxe and that sufficed. The exhilaration of the hunt was followed by the added bonus of looking through the baggage wagons drawn up in the streets of Kineton. It was an exciting day, but by the time the Cavaliers on their blown horses had hacked back to their start line they found the scene transformed. The Royalist foot had come to push of pike, but had been counter-attacked by Sir William Balfour, who with two regiments of horse had played the major part in breaking two of the brigades in the Royalist centre. But somehow or other the King and Astley had patched up a line and were still holding out. It was a pretty muddled business, and by nightfall both sides had had enough. Starving, they settled down to endure a night 'as cold as a very great frost and a sharp northerly wind could make it . . .' (Clarendon). Some of the wounded owed their lives to the fact that in that bitter weather their wounds congealed.

Despite Balfour's success it does not seem that the Roundheads were likely to end the war with a single stroke at Edgehill. The Royalists, on the other hand, had they been able to restrain their victorious cavalry, might well have destroyed the enemy. A great

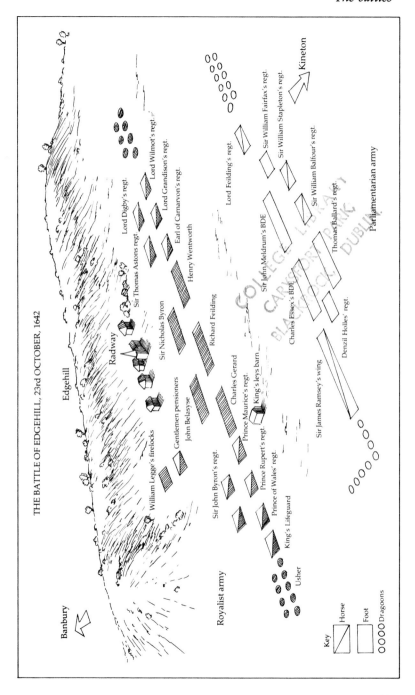

THE BATTLE OF EDGEHILL, 23rd OCTOBER, 1642

Banbury

Edgehill

Radway

Royalist army

William Legge's firelocks
Gentlemen pensioners
John Belasyse
Sir John Byron's regt.
Charles Gerard
Prince Maurice's regt.
King's ley's barn
Prince Rupert's regt.
Prince of Wales' regt.
King's Lifeguard

Usher

Sir Nicholas Byron
Sir Thomas Astons regt.
Lord Digby's regt.
Lord Wilmot's regt.
Lord Grandison's regt.
Earl of Carnarvon's regt.
Henry Wentworth
Richard Feilding

Lord Feilding's regt.
Sir John Meldrum's BDE
Charles Essey's BDE

Sir William Fairfax's regt.
Sir William Stapleton's regt.
Sir William Balfour's regt.
Thomas Ballard's regt.
Denzil Holles' regt.
Sir James Ramsey's wing

Kineton

Parliamentarian army

Key
Horse
Foot
OOOO Dragoons

69

chance was lost. The battle is often regarded as a draw, but Essex, by quitting the field, admitted defeat. He left Charles seven of his guns and allowed him to take Oxford unopposed and there set up his capital and headquarters for the next four years.

Several strange episodes happened during the battle. When Sir Nicholas Byron's Brigade was broken Sir Edmund Verney, the standard-bearer was struck down by Ensign Arthur Young; the Banner Royal fell into the hands of the rebels, and was carried to the rear. Fortunately, Sir Charles Lucas had rallied 200 Royalist cavalry and with these he charged the right flank and rear of the Roundhead Army, and one of his body, Captain John Smith, after taking a colour of Lord Wharton's Regiment, came upon six horsemen escorting a foot soldier carrying their trophy to the rear. 'Captain Smith! Captain Smith, they are carrying away the standard!' cried a boy, who knew him, and for some unexplained reason had got into the rear of the Roundhead host. 'They shall have me with it, if they carry it away!' quoth Smith and shouting, 'Traitor, deliver the standard!' set about the enemy. It is hardly surprising that they managed to wound him, but he was no mean swordsman, he killed one Roundhead, wounded another and put the rest to flight. The rebels had retained their best trophy for a bare five minutes. Not content with this exploit Smith rescued a captive brigadier, Colonel Richard Feilding. These VC acts won him a knighthood. It could scarcely have been better earned.

Two future kings hazarded their persons on the field of Edgehill: King Charles II (1630–85) and King James II (1633–1701). Balfour's troopers got within half musket shot of them and the twelve-year-old Prince Charles was heard shouting, 'I fear them not!' as he wound up his wheel-lock pistol. A Roundhead 'lobster' came careering down upon him to be received by Sir John Hinton, who could not pierce his armour with his sword. Miles Mathewes, a gentleman pensioner, came up and finished the business with his poleaxe, covering the Prince's retreat.

James II, an experienced soldier if an indifferent king, took a great deal of interest in his first battle, questioning, with youthful enthusiasm, such eyewitnesses as he met. He left a singularly lucid account of the fight, in which he makes this shrewd comment on the steadiness which has long been the most prized characteristic of the British infantry: 'Tis observed that of all nations the English stick the closest to their Officers, and its hardly seen that our common Soldiers will turn their backs, if they who commanded them do not first show them the bad

example, or leave them unofficer'd by being kill'd themselves upon the place.'

There was nothing very subtle about the tactics of Edgehill. A simple assault, followed by a counterthrust, with neither side finding any fresh formed body of troops to clinch the deal. It is true that Essex was joined towards nightfall by a few troops of horse, including Oliver Cromwell's, and by Colonel John Hampden's Brigade of Foot, but he had not the nerve or the imagination to launch them in an effort to shatter the brittle Royalist array.

It cannot be said that Charles and Essex did much better when they met on Wash Common above Newbury on 20 September 1643. Once again Charles was between Essex and his base, London, and since he now had a much better trained army than the one he had led eleven months earlier, he might reasonably have been expected to win a conclusive victory.

	King	*Essex*
Horse	6,000	4,000
Foot	8,000	10,000
Guns	20	. . .
	14,000	14,000

The siege of Gloucester had compelled Essex to hazard his army far from home, and after relieving the town the

Parliamentarians had been delayed by Rupert in an action at Aldbourne Chase, and compelled to cross to the south bank of the Kennet (18 September). But though the King reached Newbury before Essex, he and his generals failed to occupy the high ground south-west of the town in good time, though they put some cavalry outposts there. The consequence was that early next day Essex managed to establish himself on the vital ground west of Wash Common.

Part of the battlefield is now covered with modern housing, but a good idea of the ground can be obtained if you turn off the Newbury–Andover road at The Gun Inn and go westwards towards the road junction near Wash Farm. Here there is a track running north from which one can get a good view of the ground between Round Hill and the River Kennet, though it seems that this was much more enclosed then than now.

Pushing on past Cope Hall and northwards via Skinner's Green there is a good view of Round Hill from about the road and railway junction on the Enborne–Newbury road.

De Gomme has not left us a map of First Newbury. It may be suspected that the Royalists deployed their brigades as they came up and that in their hurry they failed to produce a formal order of battle. However that may be, there is little trace of much planning on either side. Rupert, after three charges, swept Sir Philip Stapleton and the right wing of the Roundhead horse from Wash Common. Sir Nicholas Byron, supported by his hard-fighting nephew, Sir John, made a fierce attack on Round Hill, but after clearing several enclosures, they were held up short of their objective. It was in this fighting that Lord Falkland was killed. Byron describes his tragic death:

> I went to view the ground, and to see what way there was to that place where the enemy's foot was drawn up, which I found to be enclosed with a high quick hedge and no passage into it, but by a narrow gap through which but one horse at a time could go and that not without difficulty. My Lord of Falkland did me the honour to ride in my troop this day, and I would needs go along with him, the enemy had beat our foot out of the close, and was drawn up near the hedge; I went to view, and as I was giving orders for making the gap wide enough, my horse was shot in the throat with a musket bullet and his bit broken in his mouth so that I was forced to

call for another horse; in the meanwhile my Lord Falkland (more gallantly than advisedly) spurred his horse through the gap, where both he and his horse were immediately killed.

Skippon brought up some regiments of the London Trained Bands which managed to hold the centre of the Parliamentarian line, behaving admirably in their first serious action.

The day's fighting ended in a stalemate, but when dawn came Essex's astonished eyes beheld a charming sight: the Royalist position had been abandoned. The Parliamentarians lost no time in pushing on to Reading and safety.

Why, you may well ask, did the Royalists quit the field? The official explanation was that they had practically run out of powder. They had sent to Oxford for fresh supplies, but too late. One wonders what would have happened if they had bluffed it out, adopting a defensive posture, and daring the cautious and lethargic Essex to try his luck in a general assault.

At the road junction near The Gun public house stands a monument to the learned and high-minded Lucius Cary, second Viscount Falkland (*c.* 1610–43), whose death, so near akin to suicide, left the high office of Secretary of State to George, Lord Digby (1612–77), a man of a restless disposition, and an imprudent and untrustworthy character, who gradually gained a great ascendancy over his royal master's mind – with fatal results. The monument not only marks an excellent point from which to begin your tour of the battlefield, but serves to remind us that in war a single volley can have a truly disastrous effect, even though its victim was no soldier. If you prefer to make your progress from ale-house to ale-house, well, there is The Gun public house just opposite, where I have refreshed myself with a flagon in times past.

It may be that thus far you will not have formed a very high opinion of the tacticians of the Civil Wars, but up and down the country good men were coming to the front: Hopton and Waller, Rupert and Maurice, Goring and Fairfax, Cavendish and Cromwell. All these had good successes to their credit, some at least of which displayed a real flair for tactics and leadership. Rupert with Powick Bridge (23 September 1642); the storming of Cirencester (2 February); the siege of Lichfield (April); the Chalgrove Raid (17/18 June) and the storming of Bristol (26 July 1643) would, in a modern army, have had a chestful of medals by this time, and he had shown, moreover, that he was much more

The Falkland Monument, Newbury. (*Radio Times Hulton Picture Library*)

than a mere sabreur: he could conduct a siege in masterly fashion – it was not for nothing that he had been at Breda in 1637. Maurice and Goring had been there too. The latter had worsted Sir Thomas Fairfax, no mean opponent, when with 800 horse he fell upon him at Seacroft Moor, inflicting 1,000 casualties (30 March 1643). Goring had been a colonel of foot in the Dutch Army and in the Bishops' War. In the Civil War he made his name as a cavalry general.

Charles Cavendish (1620–43), second son of the Earl of Devonshire, had served a campaign under the Prince of Orange, and had greatly distinguished himself at Edgehill. He quickly became Lieutenant-General of the Horse in Newcastle's army, and was very active in Nottinghamshire and Lincolnshire. He defeated the younger Hotham at Ancaster Heath (11 April 1643) and was with the Queen when her army stormed Burton-on-Trent (1 July). His meteoric career came to an early end when, in an attempt to relieve Gainsborough, his regiment was broken by Cromwell's Ironsides, and he was himself run through by Captain-Lieutenant James Berry (28 July).

Colonel Cromwell had already scored a minor success at Grantham (13 May). In this action at Gainsborough he carried out a most difficult operation. Finding himself faced by an overwhelming force of Cavaliers, he withdrew his men by alternate squadrons and got clear away. This demanded real discipline, and indeed seems to be the only recorded instance of such a manœuvre in all the annals of the Civil War. Usually when one side or the other thought things were going badly they quit the field as if trying to win a horse race. It took a level-headed man to gather a party and cover the withdrawal. Hopton managed to do this after the Royalist cavalry failed at Cheriton and its generals, Lord John Stuart and Sir John Smith, were mortally wounded.

> By this time the whole horse were in disorder, and the Lo: Hopton had much adoe to gett to the number of 300 horse to stand with him at the entrance into the Common, where all the Enemye's horse stood in bodyes before him; The greater part of that little number of horse that stayed with him were of the Queene's Regiment, where Monsr. de Plurie [Captain Raoul ffleury] theire cheife Commander doing his duty like a very worthy person in the head of them had his legg shott off to the anckle with a great shott, whereof he shortly after dyed, and the Lo: Hoptons horse received a muskett shott in the shoulder. Yet it pleased God that they made that stand good, till, with the advice, and assistance of the Earle of Brainford, the rest of the horse and foote were retreated, and had recovered the top of the Hill, where they had at first drawn up in the morning. (Hopton)

It was a pity that Hopton was not present to pick up the bits after Naseby . . . but that is another story.

Hopton was a vigilant and resourceful commander as skilful in attack as in defence. Nobody could handle a small battle, like Stratton, better than he. Whether he would have been equally at

home with an army of 10,000 or 14,000 we cannot say, for at the big battles of 1644 in which he was engaged he did not exercise supreme command. Lord Forth, not Hopton, was the overall commander at Cheriton, even though he left much of the work to his colleague.

Hopton's handling of infantry, as exemplified by Launceston, Stratton and Lansdown, seems to me exemplary. With the possible exception of Montrose he was the only one of the Civil War commanders who habitually worked round the enemy's flanks, as opposed to simply setting to partners and trusting to an all-out frontal attack.

But if the tactics of our ancestors seem horribly obvious, one must bear in mind the difficulties they laboured under. Seldom if ever did they have a settled HQ or command post. The generals simply sat on their horses, not very far from the front line, and commanded from the saddle. They thought nothing of hurling themselves into the mêlée, often with disastrous results. One wonders where the Cavalier generals sought orders and inspiration when Prince Rupert was hiding in that famous beanfield at Marston Moor.

There were a few engineers, who could make maps to show the order of battle, or the lines at a siege. But no effort was made to issue maps to all the senior officers. Finding one's way about England with the aid of Mr Speed's maps may have been just possible, but there were no maps which gave much idea of the ground and its tactical features.

A certain number of 'perspective glasses' were available, and these probably sufficed for the identification of a distant body of troops as friend or foe. By counting the number of colours you might get some idea of the strength of the formation in question. Watches were by no means commonplace, and the idea of synchronizing them lay in the future.

Let us suppose that an army is deployed in the simplest order, with foot and guns in the centre and horse on the flanks, under a general whose subordinates have been briefed for an attack. The question remains: *How do we get them going*? A possible answer would be that the general rode up to his main battery, half a dozen guns perhaps, and ordered a resounding salvo. Hopefully, all the guns would go off simultaneously, with a very loud bang. The brigade commanders and the colonels, recognizing their cue, would then advance their colours, the drums would then beat and with slow pomp of horse and foot the redcoats and the bluecoats, the greencoats and the yellowcoats; the whitecoats and the greycoats would advance upon the foe.

There was now not very much for the general to do save to set himself at the head of his lifeguard, somewhere where he could see what was happening, and where he could get hold of his reserve with the minimum of delay. The prettiest plan of an order of battle could not survive for more than a few minutes once the regiments had crossed the start line. Soon clouds of smoke descended upon the field as salvo succeeded salvo, and volley followed volley: soon it would be difficult to perceive whether the right wing had won, whether the left wing had been routed. Was the reserve needed? Was it too soon? Should he reinforce success or try to plug a gap in his battle array? Even if things went well unexpected situations could arise, as when at Edgehill the Royalist wings met with practically no resistance at all. It would not be unnatural if both Rupert and Wilmot were expecting a hard tussle, with the second line coming up after a time to reinforce the first. No such thing happened. Wilmot easily overcame Lord Feilding's single regiment. Ramsey's men, after one volley at long range, turned their horse's heads and took off for Kineton as if the Devil was after them – as in a sense he was. What chance had Rupert to make a new plan? How was he to stop Byron, who was certainly fierce and possibly a bit thick, from galloping after such an easy prey? And were Byron's newly raised troops – he had only begun to raise his regiment two months earlier – capable of checking their mounts and executing a neat left wheel, preparatory to setting about the left wing of Essex's infantry? I doubt it.

How long does it take to train a soldier? You tell me! Given willing, healthy and literate recruits aged about seventeen to thirty I will make you some reasonable infantry soldiers in a very short time indeed – but I shall need some decent NCOs – and you must not expect them to do difficult things like night ops. But cavalry! That was a very different thing, even with Cavaliers, who had ridden since childhood and brought their own horses, as many must have done. It takes time to accustom the horses to bangs, to drums and to colours. Some of them never appreciate these things. Then you must make them move about in rank and file, and if you believe that is an easy matter you will believe anything.

When Richard Atkyns made up his mind to go to the wars, he had a servant named Erwing, a Scot, who had served in the Gendarmes of the *Maison du Roi*. This good fellow had declined a lieutenant's place on the rebel side. Atkyns writes: 'Him I employed to train up my horse, and make them bold. . . .' Not all those, who went careering across the field of Edgehill on 23 October 1642, had been as prudent!

Note

1. Towton, fought on 29 March 1461, during the Wars of the Roses, may have been bigger.

CHAPTER 6

Siege warfare

My years had not amounted full eighteen,
Till I in field wounded three times had been,
Three times in sieges close had been immured,
Three times imprisonment's restraint endured.

Anthony Cooper[1]

The sieges of the Civil Wars were so numerous that in all probability a complete list of them would be well-nigh impossible to compile. In the offensive of the New Model Army, as we shall see (Ch. 9) there were something like forty-six sieges of one sort and another. They varied in importance from those of places like Bristol, and Exeter, Oxford and Worcester, to the capture of little garrisons like Bletchington House or Radcot Fort. The sieges conducted by the New Model, important though they were, were not more numerous than those undertaken by the forces under Lord Fairfax, Sir William Brereton, Sydenham Poyntz and others.

Few of the fortresses of the Civil Wars have disappeared as completely as Lathom House which has only recently been rediscovered. Generally speaking the warriors of those days were content to improve upon earlier buildings, many dating from before the introduction of gunpowder, but still visible today. The castles built by King Edward I were invaluable to the Cavaliers of North Wales, nor were the white walls of York or the red walls of Chester to be despised. Sometimes the artillery fortresses of King Henry VIII, built for coast defence, found a use which their designer had not intended. Pendennis and St Mawes are examples. Nor, of course, had the pious founders built St Chad's Cathedral and its Close in order to keep out Roundheads.

Here and there as at Warwick Castle, Basing House and Donnington Castle one can still discern bastions and bulwarks begun in 1642 or 1643 to improve upon earlier building. We have fairly good contemporary maps of some of the towns that were besieged; Plymouth, Oxford and Newark-on-Trent, but only at the last can one still see a wide range of seventeenth-century earthworks. These include the magnificent Queen's Sconce. If they are still intact it is only due in part to the historical sense of successive generations of city fathers. When the place surrendered in 1646 the Parliamentarians intended to slight it, and the country people were brought in to do the work. Happily for us the plague was abroad in Newark, and the fearful peasants hastened home – pausing only to collect their pay. (I invented that last bit, but it seems not unlikely.) In 1964 the Royal Commission on Historical Monuments (England) compiled a complete description entitled *The Siege-works at Newark-upon-Trent* (in which they invited the collaboration of the present writer). I trust that those of you, who study the Civil War sieges, will go and stay in Newark – and, if you can get a copy of the work named above, will trudge the environs of Newark, and think a little of the feats of arms done there by our kith and kin in times past. If you have a spark of historical imagination or indeed common patriotism you will not regret it, and bigoted Royalist though I am, I include stout-hearted Roundheads in this exhortation! In passing I may say that of the four Royalist governors of Newark only one has my approval, the last: Lord John Belasyse. Sir John Henderson, a Scot, I would not trust very far; Sir Richard Byron, younger brother of 'the bloody Braggadoccio' was a man of a narrow soul – I have it on the authority of that worthy antiquary Colonel Gervase Holles of Grimsby. As for Sir Richard Willys of Fen Ditton, Cambridge-shire, you have but to study his portrait by Dobson to read his character, and if you do not perceive a haughty, arrogant, self-satisfied bastard, you are no judge! It is said that during the Interregnum he used to betray the secrets of the Sealed Knot to John Thurloe (1616–68), Cromwell's Secretary of State.

One may suppose that there were but few engineers in England when the armies took the field in 1642. Prince Rupert, keen professional that he was, took the precaution of bringing over with him a Walloon engineer, Bernard de Gomme (1620–85), and a French 'fireworker', Bartholomew de la Roche, when he joined his uncle in 1642. They remained with him throughout the war, and evidence that they earned their keep is not lacking. But

Basing House, photographed from the south. Cromwell stormed the place from this direction on 14 October 1645. The Grange, scene of fierce fighting on 7 November 1643, can be seen, top left. The trace of the seventeenth-century earthworks south of the house can be clearly seen. (*Aerofilms Limited*)

who else was there? One may suppose that experienced officers like Sir Jacob Astley and Will. Legge, the Master of the Royal Armouries, could devise a fortification if need were. Military engineering can be a bit of a 'juju'. In the nature of things the Royal Engineers, right down to our own day, will never admit that anyone outside the corps could put a place in a state of defence. But I promise you I can name stupid old infantrymen, who have shown themselves not altogether incapable of that sort of work. I have seen a handsome map of the siege of Maastricht (1632) done by Ensign Charles Lloyd (*c.* 1612–78), clearly an officer of foot in the Dutch Army. This worthy next turns up as first captain in the Earl of Northumberland's Regiment of Foot in 1640. No doubt he had seen that famous siege of Breda in the meanwhile. In 1643 we find him a colonel of foot vice another Welsh worthy, Sir Thomas Salusbury, and in 1644 he is Engineer and Quartermaster-General of the Oxford Army, and then Governor of Devizes. This is a career which seems to show that the professional soldiers of the mid-seventeenth century were versatile creatures. But there simply were not enough of them to go round. The Scot, Colonel James Wemyss (*c*. 1610–67), who commanded Waller's artillery at Cropredy Bridge (29 June 1644), where the Royalists not only took eleven guns, but the chief gunner also, is also described as 'that excellent engineer'. *Mercurius Aulicus* reported that Wemyss, 'being brought before his Majestie, said, *Gud feith his heart was alwayes with His Majestie'*, adding with a nice touch of malice 'so is mine with the State-Committee', meaning the Committee of Both Kingdoms, the body which sat at Derby House in London, and ran the Parliamentarian armies by remote control.

At the outbreak of the Civil War, Johan Rosworm, a German engineer, who had seen service in the Thirty Years War and in Ireland, was living in Manchester. The principal citizens, who supported the cause of Parliament, lived in some dread of their powerful neighbour, the Royalist Lord Strange, later (29 September) Earl of Derby. And so they contracted with Rosworm to defend the town for the next six months for £30. The very next day Lord Strange sent him £150, but 'valuing honesty more than gold', as a good mercenary should, Rosworm declined the gift.

In September 1642 Lord Strange mustered 4,000 men at Warrington. Rosworm had posts and chains put up to keep out horse, and built mud walls at the ends of the streets, and this was done by 23 September. Next day the Royalists laid siege to the town, but their losses were relatively severe and on 1 October they raised their siege. Derby sent three regiments to join the King, so there followed a lull until 24 December when Rosworm made a three-day sortie designed to prevent a second siege. On 2 January 1643 Rosworm was made Lieutenant-Colonel of Colonel Ashton's Regiment of Foot, with which he took part in the successful assault on Preston (9 January). He was selected to fortify the place.

Goodrich Castle, the Royalist stronghold of Colonel Henry Lingen, who held out until 31 July 1646. (*Crown Copyright – reproduced with the permission of the Controller of Her Majesty's Stationery Office*)

In March 1643 the Mancunians persuaded Rosworm to sign a new contract. He was to have a salary of £60 per annum, to be paid quarterly during the life of himself and his wife. In return he was to complete the fortifications, and to be responsible for everything to do with the safety of the town. He agreed to resign his lieutenant-colonelcy and to accept instead command of a company of foot in the garrison of Manchester. Despite this new contract Rosworm took part in the storming of Wigan (April 1644). After its capture Colonel Holland, the Roundhead commander, left but a single company to guard 400 prisoners of war, and the captured arms and cannon. Rosworm, who escaped with all speed to Manchester, was one of those who gave evidence against Holland in the subsequent inquiry at London (15 April). He made a dangerous enemy, for Holland had powerful friends in Parliament, who were able to save him from punishment. Holland managed to stop Rosworm's pay as a captain for a year, on the grounds that he had not taken the Covenant!

In May Rosworm fortified Liverpool, but in June the place was taken by Prince Rupert. After the great Royalist victory at Adwalton Moor (29 June 1644) and the fall of Bradford, the Earl of Newcastle summoned Manchester. The citizens sent their military expert to reconnoitre and strengthen the positions at Blackstone Edge and Blackgate, by which Newcastle was expected to approach. The latter, hearing that Rosworm's defences were impregnable, abandoned the operation, and instead laid siege to Hull.

Rosworm was with Sir Thomas Fairfax in his important victory over Lord Byron at Nantwich (25 January 1644). In the autumn, as Master of the Ordnance, he directed the ten-week siege of Liverpool, which capitulated on 1 November.

While danger lasted Rosworm was in high favour with the people of Manchester, but they proved poor paymasters, and in 1648 he was compelled to go to London to seek redress. There he published a pamphlet in which he attacked the twenty-two citizens who had signed the contract with him (9 May). The advance of the Scots Army – the Engagers – induced these worthies to pay Rosworm his arrears as captain, though not his pension! Another German broadside followed. It was addressed to Sir Thomas Fairfax, John Bradshaw (1602–59) who presided over the trial of King Charles I, and Cromwell. The title of this bitter pamphlet was 'Good Service hitherto Ill-Rewarded, or An

Historicall Relation of Eight Years Service for King and Parliament in and about Manchester and those parts' (London, 1649). On 9 July Bradshaw advised the town council to pay up, but they preferred to save their money. The unlucky officer's wife and children had to be relieved by strangers, as he revealed in yet another broadside: 'The Case of Lieut. Coll. Rosworme' (July 1651). Fortunately for him the Cromwellian government proved a better employer. On 19 August 1651 Rosworm was appointed Engineer-General of all the garrisons and forts in England at 10s. a day for himself and 2s. for his clerk. His duties included a visit to New Yarmouth to select the 'fittest places for some fortification to prevent the landing of foreign forces', and a visit in September to the Isle of Man to report whether any defences were required there. On 17 April 1655 he was promoted colonel, and his pay was increased by 10s. a day, whenever he should be on actual duty. On 19 July 1659 he was appointed Engineer-General of the Army, but with the Restoration of 1660 he disappears from view. Perhaps he returned to his native Germany.

Rosworm's career, though not perhaps typical, is interesting as showing the variety of work expected of a military expert, and the difficulties he had to face.

Beyond question Newark is the best place for the study of Civil War siege engineering. Not only can the siegeworks still be seen on the ground: there are two contemporary plans, one by a Roundhead and one by a Royalist.

Newark was a very important Royalist fortress, and was besieged or assaulted several times. It was a stronghold for the Cavaliers of Nottinghamshire and Lincolnshire, and to a lesser extent Yorkshire. It was first garrisoned towards the end of 1642 and only surrendered on the King's direct order in May 1646. It controlled important communications, for there the Fosse Way, linking roads from Nottingham and Leicester with Lincoln, cuts the Great North Road at the point where it crosses the River Trent. The town was an essential link between Newcastle's northern army and the 'Oxford Army'. It was especially important in 1643, when important convoys of arms were coming into the ports of Newcastle or Scarborough and being sent south to the King. The Newarkers threatened or blockaded the communications of the Roundheads of Derby, Nottingham, Leicester and Lincoln. While the place remained in Royalist hands there was always the possibility that they would use it as a springboard for an attack on the Roundhead heartland:the Eastern Association.

The three main attacks on Newark were:

1. *27 January to 9 February 1643*: Major-General Thomas Ballard, with 6,000 men and 10 guns was repulsed by Colonel Sir John Henderson.
2. *29 February to 21 March 1644*: Sir John Meldrum besieged the town, which was relieved by Prince Rupert, the besiegers being compelled to surrender. Sir Richard Byron (1605–79) defended the place.
3. *26 November 1645 to 6 May 1646*: The Earl of Leven and Colonel-General Sydenham Poyntz besieged Newark, which was well defended by Colonel Lord John Belasyse (1614–89), who was perhaps the best soldier of the four Royalist governors of the town.

In the Newark Museum there is a very interesting plan, which shows the Royalist defences. It is drawn on vellum (30 inches by 31 inches) and in entitled: 'The Siege of Newark by the English and Scotch Armies consisting of sixteene thousand men which continued twenty and six weekes, and was surrendered the eight

Wardour Castle. The seat of Lord Arundel during the Civil Wars. It was captured by the Roundheads led by Sir Edward Hungerford in May 1643. Edmund Ludlow held out here from December 1643 until 18 March 1644, when he was compelled to surrender with his 75-strong garrison to the Royalist, Sir Francis Doddington. Lord Arundel showed Ludlow much kindness during his occupation of the castle. (*A. F. Kersting*)

of May 1646, by his Maties Commande to the Comitte of both Kingdomes for the Parliament.' Unfortunately it is neither signed nor dated. It is obviously a Royalist production for, whilst it shows the defences in detail, it gives the merest sketch of the Parliament lines. The title, too, emphasizing the length of the siege, the strength of the besiegers and the fact that the place surrendered only upon a direct order from the King, indicates a Royalist origin.

It has been suggested that the plan may have been drawn under the guidance of Sir Bernard de Gomme, but whilst, at first sight, it is not unlike his work, he was almost certainly at Oxford when it was drawn. Although details, such as the plan of the castle and the layout of the streets are neither complete nor altogether correct, the town defences, which were evidently the engineer's chief concern, give every appearance of accuracy.

Richard Clampe's plan is an engraving (20 inches by 17 inches), which covers a radius of 2 miles round Newark. It was engraved by Peregrine Lovell, and printed and sold in London by Peter Stent (who also published a picture map of Naseby). Both the British Museum and the Ashmolean at Oxford have versions of this print, the latter being the later. These two show Newark during its last siege.

Richard Clampe, who surveyed this plan, served under the Earl of Manchester and then Sir Thomas Fairfax. He was then 'before Newarke, as Engineere . . .'. He came from King's Lynn in Norfolk and was employed in the 'Custome Affaires of the said port'. In a petition of 20 December 1647 he complained to the House of Lords, that his pay was in arrears, and he needed what was due to him for 'the supply of his great necessityes'. Little is known of Peregrine Lovell, the engraver. Peter Stent, printer and publisher of engravings, maps and copy-books, worked first at the Crown and then at the sign of the White Horse in Giltspur Street between Newgate and Pye Corner from about 1643 until his death, *c*. 1667. The Ashmolean print bears the Crown address, which Stent left about 1650. It was therefore drawn very soon after the siege, and evidently represents the works of each side as they existed at the surrender. It is enlivened with little pictures of incidents during the siege, such as the hanging of a spy sent to Montrose; and the arrival of the King and Dr Hudson

The sconce, theory. From R. Ward's *Animadversions of Warre* (1639) (*National Monuments Record – Crown Copyright reserved*)

CHAP. XXXVI.

The manner of framing a Quadrangle Skonſe.

His Foure-ſquare Skonſe, is of greater ſtrength than your Triangle, and if it be favoured with a ſtrong Scituation, as great Rivers, or upon a Rocke, or where it may be flankered from the Bulworks of a Fort, it will ſtand in great ſtead ; otherwiſe it is not to be taken for a ſtrength of any moment ; The Bulworkes and Curtines are to be made very high, thicke, and ſtrong, that it may endure the battering of the Enemies Ordnance.

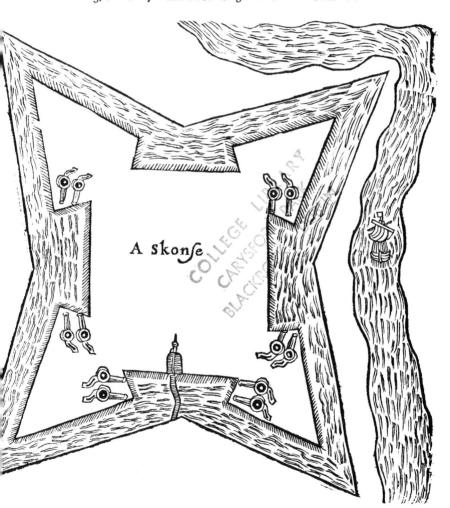

A skonſe

The Queen's Sconce at Newark viewed from the air. (*National Monuments Record – Crown Copyright reserved*)

at Kelham with an escort of the Scots, to whom they had surrendered. Cows may be seen grazing very near to the Parliamentarian lines of circumvallation.

When the Civil War began Newark was very ill prepared to resist a siege. (The same might indeed be said of most of the towns in England.) The castle survived and was still a valuable strongpoint, but the ancient mediaeval town walls, obsolete at best, had been partly destroyed as the town spread and developed north-east and south-west along the North Gate and Mill Gate. In consequence Ballard's assault very nearly got in under cover of the houses outside the North Gate. 'Sir John Henderson, the prudent Governor, caused all Northgate and that forementioned House, the Spittle, to be burned.' The Spittal, or Exeter House, which was built of stone was used by Meldrum in the 1644 siege, as his main headquarters.

The best of the surviving works is the Queen's Sconce, which lay at the Mill Gate end of the town, covering Markhall Bridge at the point where the Fosse Way crosses the River Devon. It overlooks the meadows north and west of the town, and covers an extent of about 3 acres. The earthworks are surrounded by a dry ditch, which would have had the added protection of

THE QUEEN'S SCONCE, NEWARK

The sconce, practice. The Queen's Sconce at Newark. (*National Monuments Record – Crown Copyright reserved*)

palisades, placed in the bottom of the moat in such a way that they could not be destroyed by an artillery bombardment.

Lieutenant-Colonel W. G. Ross, RE, in his 'Sieges of the Civil War', a work which is today practically unobtainable, details some of the customs of the day, which are interesting as showing how things have changed in the last 300 years. For example

91

Roundhead infantry soldiers employed on the fortifications of Worcester in September 1642, were ordered 1*s*. a day by the Earl of Essex. In other words their pay was doubled. The redcoats who, from 1726 onwards, built General George Wade's roads in the Highlands only got 6*d*. a day extra. In the wars of the present century similar work was considered to be all in the day's work.

It is worth mentioning that it was customary before laying siege to a fortress to summon the Governor to surrender. This was done with due formality by sending in a flag of truce, accompanied by drum or trumpet. Any officer worth his salt would reject the first summons with a defiant answer. Lieutenant-Colonel Roger Burges, summoned by Cromwell to surrender Faringdon Castle replied briefly, 'You are not now at Bletchingdon', a reference to the recent and over-hasty delivery of a fortified house near Oxford, whose unlucky governor paid for his failure with his life. Cromwell followed his summons with an attempt at escalade, which proved disastrous.

When the garrison was starving, or when a practicable breach had been blasted in the walls, a treaty might decently be entered into. A number of officers were appointed commissioners for either side and sat down to work out the articles for the surrender. The defenders, naturally, tried to bluff things out as best they could. They wanted to march out with the honours of war, with colours flying, drums beating and lighted match, but this was usually to expect too much.

An article was often inserted forbidding plunder or violence. There was generally an exchange of prisoners, and provision was made for the sick and wounded to be left behind until their recovery, and thereafter to be given safe conducts to return to their own party.

The Articles for the Surrender of Skipton Castle (see Appendix A), a fortress still well worth a visit, are an example of the sort of terms a dogged garrison might win for itself. For some reason the names of the Parliamentarian commissioners do not appear. Sir John Mallory (1611–56) commanded a regiment of horse and dragoons, raised at Ripon and Kirby Mallard. Sir Francis Cobb of Otringham (*c*. 1606–*c*. 1671), had commanded a troop in Prince Rupert's Regiment of Horse, before taking part in Newcastle's defence of York. Sir Ferdinando Leigh was colonel of a Yorkshire regiment of horse and Colonel John Tempest had a regiment of foot, raised in Durham.

One curious custom of those days was that, which gave the bells of a captured town to the commander of the besieging artillery – presumably he could have them recast as pieces of ordnance. On 7 August 1643 the King ordered the church wardens and parishoners of Bristol to redeem their bells, which had been forfeited because of their resistance to Prince Rupert.

One can point to instances where articles of surrender were none too scrupulously kept. This, as at Reading when Essex took it in April 1643, was usually the fault of undisciplined soldiers rather than unchivalrous officers. Still, there were hazards which a young soldier would never suspect.

Edmund Ludlow (*c.* 1617–92) after a brave defence was compelled to surrender Wardour Castle to the Royalists. The walls had been cracked by mining, and his provisions were almost at an end. When he surrendered he insisted upon quarter without distinction for the lives of everyone. The Cavaliers then found two men, who had changed sides, and despite Ludlow's protests 'were condemned and most perfidiously executed'. Captain Leicester, an officer from Ireland, who 'pretended to most experience in things of this nature, told me, that I only conditioned for my souldiers, and that these who ran from them were not mine, but theirs: . . .'. The captain was evidently 'a barrack-room lawyer'. It is little to Leicester's credit for after an unsuccessful attempt to storm the fortress Ludlow had let him carry off some of his wounded, unmolested. There were, of course, heavy-handed officers on either side, and massacres were rather more frequent than is generally realized. If Oliver Cromwell and Thomas Harrison distinguished themselves in this fashion at Basing or Drogheda, we must remember Lord Byron's 'exploit' at Barthomley Church and Sir Michael Woodhouse's at Hopton Castle.

Note

1. *Stratologia, or the History of the English Civil Warres in English Verse*, 1662. Cooper served in Lord Darcy's Regiment.

Appendix A

Skipton Castle Articles

agreed upon

Betweene Coll. RICHARD THORNETON, Commander-in-Chiefe of the forces before Skipton Castle, on the one party, and Sir JOHN MALLORY, Knight, Col. and Govenour of Skipton Castle, on the other party

about

The Surrender and Delivery of the said Castle with the Cannon, Ammunition, Goods and provisions belonging thereto, in manner after specified, to the said Coll. for the use of King and Parliament the 21st day of December,

1645.

Articles agreed upon for the surrendering of Skipton Castle to the service of the Parliament, December 21, 1645.

1. That Sir John Mallory with all the rest of the Officers, Gentlemen, and Souldiers, shall march out betwixt this and Tuesday next before twelve of the clocke, surrendering the Castle, with all the Armes, Ordnance, and Ammunition, without any prejudice done to them, with all the goods and provisions whatsoever in the said Castle, not to be purloyned or imbezzled, and whosoever shall be found offending after the sealing of these Articles for the middisposing of goods, shall be given up to Justice and treble satisfaction to be given for the goods so conveyed by the said party if he be worth it, if not, then to be made good by the Governour.

2. That all prisoners now in the Castle, of what quality of condition soever, shall be set at liberty upon the sealing of these Articles.

3. That after the signing of these Articles two such Officers as Col. Thornton shall appoint shall be admitted to go into the Castle and see the evidence house lockt up and sealed, and have an accompt of all spare Arms and Ammunition, and such a guard at such time as Col. Thornton shall appoint to goe in.

4. That the Governour, Officers, and Souldiers of Horse and Foot with their Horses and proper Arms as to horse and foot, that march out accordingly to the Honour of a Souldier, (viz.) with Colours flying, Trumpets sounding, Drums beating, Matches

lighted on both ends, and Bullets in their mouthes, every Trooper and every Foot Souldier three charges of powder, and the Officers of Commission to march with their wearing apparell that is properly their owne in their Portmantles, and not have anything taken from them, and that the Common Souldiers shall not march away with any Bag and Baggage.

5.   That all Gentlemen not in the condition of a Souldier have their horses and swords, and be allowed to march to the King or his Garrisons, or their own homes, and be protected in either condition as they shall make choyce of.

6.   That all Officers and Souldiers of Horse and Foot, Gentlemen, Townesmen, or other persons whatever belonging to this Garrison, shall have liberty, conduct and protection to go to his Majesty, or such of his Garrisons as shall be agreed of.

7.   That all Officers, Souldiers, Gentlemen, Townesmen or others, desiring to goe and live at home, shall have free leave there to remain under the protection of the Parliament.

8.   That all Souldiers or other persons that are sick or hurt, and not able to goe to their homes or other places where they desire, shall have leave to stay here at Skipton, and shall be allowed necessary accomodation untill it please God they shall recover, and then to have Passes upon their desires to goe to their home or to such of his Majestie's next Garrisons they shall make choyce of.

9.   That all women and Children within this Garrison be suffered to go with or to such as they shall desire to their own habitations.

10.   That all the hangings and other goods given in by Inventory to be the Countess of Pembroke shall be there secured by themselves and not made sale of untill the Lady of Pembroke bee made acquainted therewith, but to be prized with the rest.

11.   That all the evidences and writings whatever belonging to the Countesse of Pembroke or to the Countesse of Corke in any of the Evidence Houses of this Castle, shall not be looked into by any, untill both the Countesses be acquainted therewith, and for that end that two Moneths time for notice to be given them, and the Kayes to be delivered to Col. Thornton, who is interessed with them in the meantime.

12.   That all possible care be taken to preserve the Woods and Parks belonging to both the Ladies.

13.   That those that intend to march to his Majesty or any of his Garrisons march but six miles a day, and free Quarter during all their March, and that a sufficient Convoy be allowed them, and may conduct them to Nottingham, and from thence to one of these foure Garrisons as shall be there named by them to the Commander in Chiefe of the Convoy, viz., Banbury, Worcester, Hereford or Litchfield.

14.   That if any persons belonging to this Garrison shall misdemean themselves in the march, it shall not extend further than the parties offending, upon whom Justice shall be done according to the fault committed.

15.   That if any Officers or Souldiers shall be necessitated to buy horses, or anything else in their march, shall have liberty for that purpose, and after payment enjoyment thereof during the protection of the Convoy.

These Articles are agreed of us who were appointed to treate for the rendition of Skipton Castle, in the behalf of Sir John Mallory, Govenour of Skipton.

FERDINANDO LEIGH.   FRAN. COBB.
JOHN TEMPEST.   MICAH TOMPSON.

CHAPTER 7

The offensive of Hopton and the Cornish Army, 1643

I cannot contain myself within my doores, when the King of England's standard waves in the field upon so just occasion: the cause being such as must make all that dye in it little inferior to martyrs. And for myne owne part, I desire to acquire an honest name or an honourable grave. I never loved my life or ease so much as to shun such an occasion, wch if I should I were unworthy of the profession I have held as to succede those Ancestors of mine who have so many of them sacrificed their life for their country.

Sir Bevill Grenvile, 1640

Sir Bevill may have expressed himself better than many of his contemporaries among the Cornishmen, yet it is evident that when he wrote these lines to Sir John Trelawny, he spoke for the majority of his countrymen. Yet when in August 1642 the Commissioners of Array summoned a general muster on Bodmin racecourse only 180 men appeared, and they were for the most part Grenvile's tenants.

The arrival of Sir Ralph Hopton with 160 horse and dragoons tipped the balance, and soon the Cornish Cavaliers had a small army. On 4 October the Posse Comitatus mustered on Moilesbarrow Down and Hopton reviewed 3,000 well-armed men, and many more armed with cudgels.

King Henry VIII's fortresses, Pendennis Castle and St Mawes, which guard the mouth of the Fal, were secured by Sir Nicholas Slanning and Lieutenant Hannibal Bonython. The possession of Falmouth soon proved a great asset to the Royalists for a storm drove three Parliamentarian warships, well provided with arms and money, into the little port on 17 January 1643.

Meanwhile the Parliamentarians were sending troops to secure Plymouth. There were amphibious raids on Millbrook, where

No. 3 Commando used to train for similar activities in 1940, and in January the Parliamentarians followed this up with a full-scale invasion of Cornwall. To meet this threat the Cavaliers rendezvoused in Lord Mohun's park at Boconnoc, $2\frac{1}{2}$ miles east of Lostwithiel. Next day (19 January) they drew up on the fair heath between Braddock Church and Boconnoc. Grenvile described the Roundhead position as 'a pretty rising ground which was in the way towards Liskerd . . .'. Here Sir Ralph Hopton won the first of the victories that were to put him in the forefront of the Cavalier commanders. The Western Army was usually commanded jointly by Lord Mohun, Hopton, Sir John Berkeley and Colonel William Ashburnham, or any two of them; an odd arrangement. In this crisis they decided that one man should exercise overall command, and, though he was a Somerset man, the 'insular' Cornish chose Hopton. They could not have made a better choice. One salvo and a resolute charge by Grenvile's pikemen clinched the deal. The Roundheads, short of 1,500 prisoners, 5 guns, their baggage and their arms, were driven back across the Tamar rather quicker than they came.

There are those who will tell you that the Trained Bands, save only those of London, were virtually useless. But Braddock Down was a clear victory for the Cornish Trained Bands in the very role for which they were designed: home defence. But if they would turn out *pro aris et focis* the independent-minded Cornishmen were damned if they would be ordered abroad. If they meant to invade Devon it behoved the Cornish commanders to raise 'volutary' regiments and this they did: the five colonels, a noble band, were:

William Godolphin (*b.* 1605–)
Sir Bevill Grenvile (1596–1643)
Warwick, Lord Mohun (1620–1665)
Sir Nicholas Slanning (*c.* 1606–43)
John Trevanion (1613–43)

These men were backed by others of the principal families of the Duchy: Arundell, Bassett, Killigrew, Trelawny, Trevelyan and Vyvyan. Conservatism, loyalty, religion and tradition bound the Cornish to the Royalist cause.

Pendennis Castle, Falmouth. (*Crown Copyright – reproduced with the permission of the Controller of Her Majesty's Stationery Office*)

The coming campaign was to take a heavy toll of these gallants, as an oft-quoted rhyme tells us:

'The four wheels of Charles's wain,
Grenville, Godolphin, Trevanion, Slanning, slain.'

A Godolphin was the first to fall. He was not the colonel of foot, but Sidney Godolphin (1610–43), poet and MP for the family borough of Helston. Small of stature, sensitive and retiring, he had thrown himself into the fighting with exemplary courage. On 8 February 1643 he rode in a sweep through East Devon led by Sir John Berkeley. Setting out from Plympton, they found Tavistock empty, pushed on to Okehampton and then to Chagford, a halting-place for the pack-horses which plied between Brixham and Okehampton. Berkeley's scouting was not, it seems, beyond reproach. In the cold dawn the Cavaliers clattering into the little town, came under fire, and a chance shot 'from an undiscerned and undiscerning hand', as Thomas Hobbes puts it, struck Godolphin above the knee. 'O God, I am hurt', he cried. He died in the porch of The Three Crowns. 'One losse we have sustained that is unvalluable', wrote Grenvile to his lady, 'to wit Sidney Godolphin is slaine in the attempt, who was as gallant a gent as the world had.' They buried him in Okehampton Church.

Soon after this raid a truce was concluded, and strange though it may seem, it lasted for forty days. During this time the Earl of Stamford, who was at Exeter – suffering from gout – managed to reorganize his army and by 15 April he had 3,500 foot and 8 troops of horse. He had with him moreover, a keen, young professional soldier, Major-General James Chudleigh, aged twenty-five, who had seen service in Ireland. The truce ended at midnight on 22 April, and Chudleigh lost no time in advancing on Launceston, where he received a rude reception from Hopton. The fight took place on Beacon Hill (or the Windmill) and around Polston Bridge (23 April).

The Royalists, unduly elated by their victory advanced across Sourton Down on the night of 25 April, and failing to take the proper precautions got themselves bushwhacked by Chudleigh and a squadron of cavalry. An army of 3,600 was practically routed by this enterprising handful. But Hopton was no more dismayed by this setback than Chudleigh had been by Launceston. Leaving garrisons in Saltash and Millbrook he advanced via North Pertherwin and Week St Mary to seek out the

Earl of Stamford, who had established himself on the hill, east of Bude, which bears his name. On the evening of 15 May the Cavaliers were in contact with their enemy at Efford Mill, south-west of Stratton.

Local tradition tells us that Grenvile had his HQ that night in The Tree Inn at Stratton. A copy of Sir Godfrey Kneller's painting (*c.* 1680) of Anthony Payne, the Cornish giant, who was Sir Bevill's bodyguard, may be seen there. After the Restoration he became yeoman of the guns at Plymouth. (If The Tree was not Grenvile's HQ it ought to have been for you have my assurance that it keeps a good table!)

Stamford's position is an irregular ridge, 200 feet above sea-level, running north and south, and crowned at the southern end by what looks like a small Iron Age fort. It may perhaps have served the Earl as a powder magazine. To the east the hill was steepish and wooded. With that at his back Stamford's men would be unable to retreat in good order should things go wrong. The slope towards Bude, the direction from which the Cornish might be expected to advance, was gentler, and afforded a reasonable position for the 500 Royalist cavalry, who drew up on what is now Bude Golf Course, to act as a reserve. There was nothing subtle in the way Stamford arrayed his men, perhaps he relied too much on mere numbers. And, in addition, he made the serious error of detaching Sir George Chudleigh with 1,200 of his 1,400 horse to raid Bodmin and break up a 'Posse Comitatus' which the Sheriff had summoned. This left the balance of force at Stratton:

	Hopton	Stamford
Horse	500	1,200
Foot	2,400	5,400
Guns	8	13
	2,900	6,600

It seems strange under the circumstances that the Royalists should now have won a resounding victory. Was it simply that the Cornish were better men than the Roundhead levies? Was Stamford's remote-control generalship a discouragement? It is hard to say. Certainly there was no lack of leadership on James Chudleigh's part. Late in the afternoon he led a smart counter-attack, charging the column under Sir Bevill Grenvile, who was hurled to the ground. Sir John Berkeley came to his relief in the nick of time, and in the mêlée Chudleigh was captured.

The second secret of this 'seasonable victory' was doubtless Hopton's tactics: his attack by what may be called converging battalion columns. After the failure of Chudleigh's counter-attack Slanning and Trevanion evidently rolled up Stamford's right flank. His men assailed on all sides, albeit by inferior numbers, simply did not know which way to face, and got in a confounded muddle.

Hopton describes the final phase:

> Then the enemy gave ground apace, insomuch as the four parties, growing nearer and nearer as they ascended the hill, between three and four of the clock, they all met together upon one ground near the top of the hill, where they embraced with unspeakable joy, each congratulating the other's success, and all acknowledging the wonderful blessing of God; and being there possessed of some of the enemy's cannon, they turned them upon the camp, and advanced together to perfect their Victory.

The triumphant Cornish slept where they fought, too tired to pursue. The spoils of war included: 70 barrels of powder; 1,700 prisoners; 13 guns and £5,000. There was also a great deal of food, ammunition and baggage.

The Parliamentarians lost 300 slain, and Hals the Cornish historian, records the macabre fact that thereafter the battlefield used to produce 60 bushels of corn an acre, 'the fertility whereof

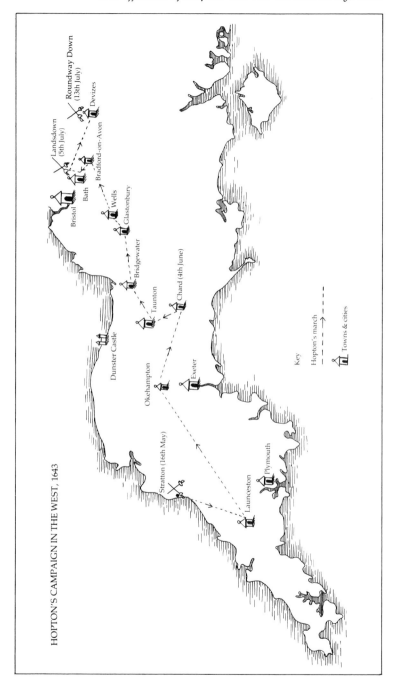

HOPTON'S CAMPAIGN IN THE WEST, 1643

Roundway Down (13th July)

Devizes

Landsdown (5th July)

Bath

Bradford-on-Avon

Bristol

Wells

Glastonbury

Bridgewater

Taunton

Chard (4th June)

Dunster Castle

Okehampton

Exeter

Stratton (16th May)

Launceston

Plymouth

Key

Hopton's march

Towns & cities

is ascribed to the virtue the land received from the blood of the slain men and horses and the trampling of their feet in this battle'.

Well might Francis Bassett write to his wife from Truro, two days later:

> Dearest Soule, Oh Deare Soule, prayse God everlastingly. Reade ye inclosed. Ring out yo' Bells. Rayse Bonefyers, publish these Joyful Tydings, Beleeve these Truthes. Excuse my writing larger. I have not tyme. We march on to meete our Victoryous ffrinds, and to sease all ye Rebells left if we can ffinde such Lyvinge. Your Dutyeous prayers God has heard, and blest us accordingly. Pray everlasting. So Jane and Betty and all you owne. I will God willing it, hasten to thee all possibly I may.

Hopton and Grenvile treated Chudleigh well for 'they loved him as a gallant enemy and one like to do the King good service if he were recovered to his loyalty' (Clarendon). Disgusted by the flight of Stamford's army he now changed sides, writing to his father 'on the faith and honour of a gentleman and a soldier, I never saw any army freer from vice, nor more religiously inclined than I perceive the whole genius of this Army to be.' This opinion of the Cornish Army was published in a pamphlet, preserved in the Bodleian Library, entitled 'Sergeant-Major James Chudleigh his Declaration to his Countrymen'.

This astonishing army now made a strategic move well-nigh incredible in so 'insular' a nation as the Cornish. Ignoring the fact that Bideford and Barnstaple, Exeter and Plymouth, were all in Parliamentarian hands, they marched right through Devonshire and joined hands at Chard (4 June) with an army brought from Oxford by the Marquis of Hertford and Prince Maurice.

	Maurice	Hopton	Total
Horse	1,500	500	2,000
Dragoons	—	300	300
Foot	1,000	3,000	4,000
Guns	11	5	16
	2,500	3,800	6,300

In the days before wireless that was not a bad strategic combination. Unhappily, there were discordant elements in this handsome little marching army.

Hopton complains of Maurice's cavalry:

> There began the disorder of the horse visibly to break in upon
> all the prosperity of the public proceedings. The Town
> [Taunton] agreeing willingly to raise and pay £8,000
> composition (which would have sufficed for some weeks
> necessary pay for the whole Army;) The Country being then
> full, and not relucting at free-quarter soberly taken, . . . [the
> generals were] never able to represse the extravagant
> disorder of the horse to the ruin and discomposure of all.

On the other hand Captain Richard Atkyns, who belonged to
one of the best regiments, Prince Maurice's, wrote that 'the
Cornish foot could not well brook our horse (especially, when we
were drawn up upon corn) but they would many times let fly at
us: these were the very best foot I ever saw, for marching and
fighting; but so mutinous withal, that nothing but an alarm could
keep them from falling upon their officers'. Certainly it needed
heavy-handed officers to keep an army like this in good order.

Though many of the Royalist commanders were loved by their
men for their brave leadership, one may be permitted to doubt
whether as disciplinarians they were strict enough. But how can
you discipline soldiers, whether of British or any other race
unless they are kept in constant pay? This in a nutshell was the
chief problem of the Royalist armies.

Settling a garrison in Taunton, a town very ill disposed, then
and later, to the Stuart monarchy, the Western Army pushed on
to Glastonbury and Wells, where they had tidings of a fresh
enemy: Sir William Waller, alias 'William the Conqueror' or 'the
Night Owl', an officer of much higher calibre than my gouty
ancestor. Waller made a stand on the Mendip Hills in order to
cover Bath, and there on 10 June a strange fight took place at
Chewton Mendip, a little place 5 miles from Wells and some 12
miles from Bath. Atkyns describes what took place:

> . . . When we came to Wells, intelligence was given us, that
> Sir William Waller's army was drawn out on that side of Bath;
> we marched toward them as far as Chuton, which I suppose,
> is about half way; the Sun was then about an hour high, and
> many of our horse and foot tired with our march; so the foot
> had orders to quarter at Wells, as the headquarters, and the
> horse thereabouts: The quarter-masters were sent to take up

quarters accordingly; and the Lord Carnarvan with this
regiment of horse, went to give their whole army an alarm;
but came so near them, that for haste, they sent out a fresh
regiment of horse, and another of dragoons to fight him; his
Lordship's regiment being much wasted, and his horses tired
with the long march were forced to retreat; and the enemy
had the pursuit of them to Chuton, where Prince Maurice
was hurt, and taken prisoner. We were then a mile on our
way towards our quarters, when Colonel Brutus Bucke
acquainted our regiment with this unwelcome news; which I
heard first, having the honour to command the rear division
of the regiment. My Lieutenant-Colonel [Guy Molesworth],
my Major [Thomas Sheldon], and the rest of the officers,
advised what to do in this case; and the result was, that
Prince Maurice having himself commanded his regiment to
their quarters, they were subject to a Council of War, if they
should disobey command; to which I answered (being eldest
[i.e. senior] captain) that I was but a young soldier, and if
they would give me leave, I would draw off my division and
run the hazard of a Council of War; they told me, they might
as well go themselves, as give me leave to go; but if I would
adventure, they would not oppose it, but defend me the best
they could.

I drew off my division with all possible speed, and put
them in order, which were not above 100 men; and before we
had marched twelve score yards, we met the Lord
Carnarvan's regiment scattered, and running so terribly, that
I could hardly keep them from disordering my men (though
in a large champaign) at last I met his Lordship with his horse
wellnigh spent, who told me I was the happiest sight he ever
saw in his life: I told him I was no less glad to see his
Lordship; for as yet I had no command for what I had done,
and now I hoped he would give me command publicly, to
preserve me from the censures of a Council, which he did.
The enemy seeing a party make towards them left their
pursuit, and drew up at Chuton, and the Lord Carnarvan,
the Lord Arundel of Wardour, with myself, marched in the
head of my party; this was about half an hour before sunset;
and when we came within 20 score of the enemy, we found
about 200 dragoons half musket shot before a regiment of
horse of theirs in two divisions, both in order to receive us. At
this punctilio of time, from as clear a sunshine day as could be

seen, there fell a sudden mist, that we could not see ten yards off, but we still marched on; the dragoons amazed with the mist, and hearing our horse come on; gave us a volley of shot out of distance, and disordered not one man of us, and before we came up to them, they took horse and away they run, and the mist immediately vanished. We had then the less work to do, but still we had enough; for there were 6 troops of horse in 2 divisions, and about three or four hundred dragoons more, that had lined the hedges on both sides of their horse; when we came within 6 score of them, we mended our pace, and fell into their left division, routing and killing several of them.

The dragoons on both sides, seeing us so mixed with their men that they could not fire at us, but they might kill their own men as well as ours; took horse and away they run also. In this charge, I gave one Captain [Edward] Kitely quarter twice, and at last he was killed: the Lord Arundel of Wardour also, took a dragoon's colours, as if it were hereditary to the family so to do; but all of us overran the Prince, being prisoner in that party; for he was on foot, and had a hurt upon his head, and I suppose not known to be the Prince. My groom coming after us, espied the Prince, and all being in confusion, he alighted from his horse, and gave him to the Prince, which carried him off: and though this was great success, yet we were in as great danger as ever; for now we were in disorder and had spent our shot; and had not time to charge again; and my Lieutenant [Thomas Sandys] and Cornet [Robert Holmes], with above half the Party, followed the chase of those that ran, within half a mile of their army; that when I came to rally, I found I had not 30 men; we had then three fresh troops to charge, which were in our rear; but by reason of their marching through a wainshard [waggon yard] before they could be put in order: I told those of my party, that if we did not put a good face upon it, and charge them presently, before they were in order, we were all dead men or prisoners; which they apprehending, we charged them; and they made as it were a lane for us, being as willing to be gone as we ourselves. In this charge there was but one of my troop killed, and 8 hurt. For the wounded men of my troop, and also of my division I received 20s. a man of Sir Robert Long, then Treasurer of the Army; which was all the money I ever received for myself, or troops, during the war.

When I came to Wells, the headquarters; I was so weary that I did not my duty to the Prince that night, but laid me down where I could get quarters; I was much unsatisfied for the loss of my Lieutenant and Colours, of which I had then no account; and laid all the guards to give me news of them, if they escaped. Early in the morning Mr Holmes my Cornet brought my Colours to me, which pleased me very well; but with this allay, that my Lieutenant Thomas Sandys, my near kinsman was taken prisoner, and one more gentleman of my troop with him; and that he with some few troopers, took such leaps that the enemy could not follow them, else they had been taken also. The next morning I waited upon Prince Maurice, and presented him with a case of pistols, which my Uncle Sandys brought newly out of France; the neatest that I ever saw, which he then wanted; but as yet he knew not the man that mounted him, nor whose horse it was; when I saw the horse I knew him, and the man that rid him that day; who was the groom aforesaid: the Prince told me he would not part with the horse, till he saw the man that horsed him, if he were alive, and commanded me to send him to him; which I did that day, and when he came to the Prince, he knew him, and gave him 10 broad pieces, and told him withal, that he should have any preferment he was capable of. This graceless fellow went from my troop, and took two troopers with him, none of which ever returned again: about 15 years after [1658?] I saw him begging in the streets of London, with a muffler before his face, and spake inwardly, as if he had been eaten up with the foul disease. . . .

This description seems to conjure up the hack and gallop cavalry actions of those days in a marvellously evocative way.

The fighting that followed was of a very different nature. After endless manœuvrings, with two skilful generals ever seeking to catch the other in an unguarded moment, a daring sortie brought on a general action, in which the Cavaliers stormed Lansdown Hill, north of Bath.

Waller's army was drawn up on the crest of the hill with breastworks of earth and fascines, manned by musketeers, and with cannon planted at intervals. Bodies of horse and foot were drawn up in support of this front line. 'Thus fortified', wrote the Royalist, Lieutenant-Colonel Walter Slingsby, 'stood the fox gazing at us when our whole army was ranged in order of battle upon the large cornfield near Tughill.'

It was a formidable position, and the Cavaliers cannot be blamed if they did not like the look of it. Seeing them retreat Waller sent Colonel Burrell with 1,000 horse and foot to harass their flank and rear. They met with some success at first, but the Royalists fought back and by about 2 p.m. were back on the position they had quit that morning. But the situation had altered; the Cornishmen had got their blood up and were clamouring to 'fetch those cannon'. Hopton knew his men: in this mood they could perform miracles. He launched them to the attack, sending out strong parties of musketeers 'to gain the flank of the enemy on top of the hill . . .'. As at Launceston and Stratton he demonstrated his belief in worrying the enemy by working on his flanks: he had a real flair for modern tactics! Once the musketeers were on their way Sir Bevill Grenvile's pikes, supported by Royalist cavalry made a frontal attack more or less up the axis of the Marshfield–Bath road. A hard bout followed and it is wonderful that the Royalists reached the top at all. The explanation is perhaps that the very steepness of the hill gave them a measure of cover in 'dead ground'. Roundhead musketeers, aiming down the hill, were compelled to expose their bodies from the waist upwards. As salvo followed salvo, battle smoke formed a screen of a kind. Captain Richard Atkyns has left a vivid description of the scene.

As I went up the hill, which was very steep and hollow, I met

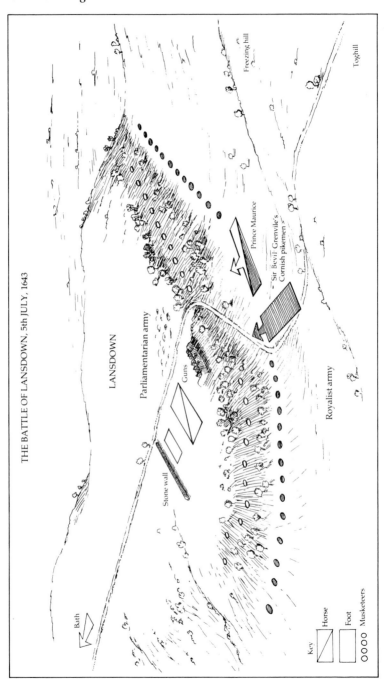

THE BATTLE OF LANSDOWN, 5th JULY, 1643

Freezing hill

Toghill

Prince Maurice

Sir Bevil Grenvile's
Cornish pikemen

LANSDOWN

Parliamentarian army

Royalist army

Guns

Stone wall

Bath

Key

Horse

Foot

OOOO Musketeers

several dead and wounded officers brought off; besides several running away, that I had much ado to get up by them. When I came to the top of the hill, I saw Sir Bevill Grinvill's stand of pikes; which certainly preserved our army from total rout, with the loss of his most precious life: they stood as upon the eaves of an house for steepness but as unmovable as a rock; on which side of their stand of pikes our horse were, I could not discover for the air was so darkened by the smoke of the powder that for a quarter of an hour together (I dare say) there was no light seen, but what the fire of the volleys of shot gave; . . .

You may readily find the exact spot where Grenvile fell for it is marked by a handsome obelisk erected by his son, John Grenvile, first Earl of Bath (1628–1701), who, as a boy of thirteen fought there. When his father fell his giant retainer, Anthony Payne, is said to have hoisted him into the saddle, so that, with a Grenvile still at its head, this brave regiment would hold its ground, amidst the volleys of shot and the constant charges of Roundhead horse. The cavalry charges were probably easier for the pikemen to endure than the musketry, for the horsemen, fearful of breaking their necks by galloping over the edge, could not really get up speed.

Gradually Hopton was able to consolidate his grip on the lip of the steep hillside, and Waller, his flanks plagued by musketeers, drew back to a stone wall some 400 yards to his rear.

Hopton's position was still an unenviable one for not 600 of his 2,000 horse were still with him. Some had fallen, others rode horses that could no longer raise a trot let alone a canter. Many, if Clarendon is to be believed, had fled. Some did not draw rein until they reached Oxford where they 'according to the custom of those who run away, reported all to be lost, with many particular accidents which they fancied very like to happen when they left the field'.

Slingsby compares the Royalist position to a 'heavy stone upon the very brow of the hill, which with one lusty charge might well have been rolled to the bottom . . .', but with the onset of night all fell quiet. Hopton and Waller each had his difficulties, and the next move depended upon the answer to a question, at once very simple and very difficult. Which general had the better nerves? It proved to be Hopton, for when the Royalist commanders gave one of the Soldiers a piece of gold to creep forward upon a one-man patrol, he found that Waller and his host had silently stolen away. The Roundheads had admitted defeat.

Lansdown proved a Pyrrhic victory, for next day a disaster of a peculiarly stupid sort took place. The Royalists put some of their prisoners into the cart which contained their ammunition. Despite a wound in the arm Hopton accompanied by a group of officers rode up to have a look at them, and the cart blew up! One of the captives had been smoking. Sir Ralph Hopton, with Major Thomas Sheldon and Cornet Wastneys, both of Prince Maurice's Regiment, and others, were blown up. 'It made a great noise and darkened the air for a time', wrote Atkyns, 'and the burnt men made lamentable screeches.' Hopton, blinded and apparently upon the point of death, was carried from the field. The same day Sir Bevill Grenvile died at Cold Ashton Parsonage.

Though not a soldier by trade Grenvile had shown a wonderful aptitude for leadership. 'No accidents', wrote Clarendon, 'could make any impression on him and his example kept others from taking anything ill or at least seeming to do so.' He was a true descendant of Sir Richard Grenvile of the *Revenge*. Well might a eulogist, M. Llwellin, write of him, 'Thy Grandsire fills the Seas, and Thou the Land.' But a letter to his widow from a friend, Sir John Trelawny of Trelawne, is better than any formal elegy, and breathes the true Cavalier spirit:

> Seeing it hath pleased God to take him from your Ladyship, yet this may something appease y^r greate fluxe of tears, that he died an Honourable Death, wch all Enemies will Envy, fighting with Invincible Valour, and Loyalty ye Battle of his God, his King, and his Country. A greater Honour than this, no man living can enjoy. But God hath called him unto himselfe, to Crowne him with Immortal Glory for his noble Constancye in this Blessed Cause.

The Royalists, in Slingsby's words, 'drooped for their Lord whom they loved'. Deprived of Hopton's leadership they quit Marshfield and made for Chippenham. Waller hearing of the change in their fortunes, followed and on 9 July caught up with them 3 miles short of Devizes. Whilst Lieutenant-Colonel Walter Slingsby, of Mohun's Regiment, fought a staunch rearguard action, probably at Rowde Ford, and the rest of the army ensconced itself in the town, Waller settled down for the night in an ancient earthwork on the summit of Roundway Down.

The Cavaliers now held a council of war at Hopton's lodging,
for, as he tells us, he was 'then not able to move himself thence
but as he was carried in a chair'. It was unanimously agreed that
the cavalry should break out that night and seek relief from
Oxford. They got away without loss, and in the nick of time for
next day Waller deployed his men within carbine-shot,
beleaguering the place on all sides and raising a battery upon a
low eminence to the east, called Coatefield.

The Cavaliers from hedges, banks and barricades showed a
bold front. 'Wee soe barocaded the Advenues', Slingsby proudly
relates, 'that theire horse could not charge in upon us, neither
durst their Foote attempt us, wee being almost twice theire
number, and better Foote.' But they were seriously short of
ammunition. Much troubled, Captain Mark Pope, the Comptrol-
ler of the Ordnance came to Hopton's bedside, and told him that
he had only 150 lb weight of match left in store. Sir Ralph, whose
brain was as clear as ever, instantly devised an expedient. He sent
a guard from house to house, gathering all the bedcords they
could lay their hands on, to be beaten and boiled in resin. This
simple device produced 1,500 lb weight of match.

113

Meanwhile Lord Crawford, coming from Oxford with a convoy of ammunition, had managed to get himself routed by Major Dowet, a French officer in the service of Parliament. On 11 July Waller sent his trumpeter to tell his opponent of this setback and to offer him reasonable terms. Hopton played for time and obtained a truce until 6 p.m. This gave his men a bit of rest, and, more important, prevented their banging away their ammunition. On the 12th rain stopped play, and gave Sir William a chance to catch up with his correspondence. To Essex at Thame he wrote urging him not to let a Royalist relief force break through. To Speaker Lenthall he wrote: 'The Cornish defend it bravely we hope that God will either scatter if not destroy this mighty army of the West; He hath wrought wonders for us, and we hope the Lord will keep us from that great strength they expect from Oxford.' He wrote in vain, for Lord Wilmot with 1,800 horse and 2 galloping guns was already at Marlborough. This news reached Waller next day, and so instead of attempting a storm, which he may have intended, he drew off his beleaguering army to a position on Roundway Down. Opinions differ as to precisely how he arrayed his men, but initially they must have been facing the place where the old Marlborough–Bath road crossed the Wansdyke. In conventional fashion he deployed with cavalry on each flank, infantry and guns in the centre. He let Wilmot cross the Wansdyke unmolested, and the Royalist commander let off his guns to let the foot in Devizes know that help was at hand. Despite Hopton's urgings they were slow to take the hint, and the battle was lost and won before ever they reached the field.

Wilmot had three brigades: his own, Sir John Byron's and Lord Crawford's, each about 600 strong. Byron wrote a good account of the fight, which was printed at York in 1643, but has scarcely been used by modern historians.

The battle began with the Roundheads sending out some troops, which Major Paul Smith (Wilmot's Regiment) forced to turn their backs.

> Sir Arthur Hazelrig seconded these with his formidable regiment of lobsters, I mean his cuirassiers whom the Lieut. General [Wilmot] intermyned with his brigade, and forced them to retreat, not so but that they rallied themselves again and charged the second time, but with worse success; for then my brigade being drawn up to second my Ld. Wilmot,

they all ran away that could, and from that time Sir Arthur Hazelrig appeared no more in the battle; upon this Waller drew his whole army down the hill, and advanced with his own brigade of horse, with two pieces of cannon before it, and two great bodies of foot on the left flank of it, these it fell to my share to charge with my brigade, my Ld. Wilmot meanwhile rallying his men together to second me if occasion should be. As I marched towards them up the hill, their cannon played upon me at a very near distance, but with very small loss, killing but two in Col. Sandyes regiment; the musketeers all this while played upon our flank, and hurt & killed some; and another regiment of their horse was watching an opportunity to charge us either in the rear or in the flank, but were hindered by Ld. Crawford. By this time we were come very near to Waller's brigade, and the command I gave my men was that not a man should discharge his pistol till the enemy had spent all his shot, which was punctually observed, so that first they gave us a volley of their carbines, then of their pistols, and then we fell in with them, and gave them ours in their teeth, yet they would not quit their ground, but stood pushing for it a pretty space, till it pleased God, (I thinke) to put new spirit into our tired horse as well as into our men, so that though it were up the hill, and that a steep one, we overbore them, and with that violence, that we forced them to fall foul upon other reserves of horse that stood behind to second them, & so swept their whole body of horse out of the field, and left their foot naked, and pursued them *near* 3 m., over the downs in Bristol way till they came to a precipice, where their fear made them so valiant that they galloped as if it had been plain ground, and many of them brake both their own and their horses' necks. In my return from the chase I took two pieces of their cannon, & divers waggons laden with ammunition, & then rallied together our scattered troops, which were as much broken as the enemy, by reason of their hot pursuit, in the meantime my Ld. Wilmot charged their foot with the horse he had with him, but could not break them, and in the charge Dudley Smith was slain, & Lt. Col. [Thomas] Weston [Digby's Regiment] hurt & many others, but when they saw my horse rallied together again before them, & the Lieut. Gen. continuing still in the rear of them, and that the Cornish foot began to sally out of the town, they thought it not fit to stay any longer, they began first gently to march off, their officers marching before them, amongst which (as I have been told since) Sir William Waller himself was, & Popham. With that I advanced towards them with those troops I had rallied, & shot at them with the cannon I had formerly taken, their officers thought it not fit to stay any longer, but such as had horses rid away as fast as they could, & too fast for us to overtake them, & the rest blew up their powder & threw down their arms & betook themselves to their heels, our horse fell in amongst them & killed 600 of them, & hurt many more, and took 800 prisoners & all their colours, & this was the success of their great conqueror.

The victory on our side as entire as possibly can be imagined, their horse & foot being totally routed, and all their cannon being 7 brass pieces taken, & all their ammunition. . . .

According to Byron, Waller's army consisted of:

	Regiments	*Numbers*
Horse	6	2,500
Dragoons	1	500
Foot	5	2,500
Cannon of brass		7
		5,500

The Roundheads lost 600 killed, 800 prisoners, 28 colours, 8 standards, the guns and ammunition and most of the arms and the baggage.

On the Royalist side few were killed, save Dudley Smith, though many officers and gentlemen were hurt. No less than 113 captives were set free including Mistress Parsons. History does not relate who she was, or why the Roundheads should have held her in durance vile. No doubt the reader's imagination will supply a suitably romantic answer!

Truly this was an astonishing battle. The Roundhead horse alone outnumbered Wilmot's men and yet he routed them. What went wrong? Perhaps the Cavaliers came in from a flank, and routed Hesilrige before the horse of Waller's right could come to their support. Maybe their infantry, instead of being a help, simply got in the way.

It was all very odd. It is not as if the Roundhead cavalry were bad units. Hesilrige's was generally considered an impressive regiment. Certainly Wilmot's men consisted largely of regiments, which had become accustomed to see the backs of their enemies ever since the days of Powick Bridge and Edgehill. But they and their horses were tired by long marches. What can one say? In war one is sometimes granted that sort of day – when simply Nothing goes Wrong. Certainly Roundway Down was Lord Wilmot's finest hour.

Poor Waller described it as 'My dismal defeat at Roundway Down.' It came at a moment when a faction intended to take the command from Essex and bestow it upon him; but, as he tells us:

> The news of this defeat arrived whilst they were deliberating on my advancement, and itt was to me a double defeat. I had nearly sunke under the affliction, but that I had a deare and sweet Comforter; and I did att that time prove according to Ecclesiasticus, chap. xxvi *'A virtuous woman rejoiceth her husband . . . As the Sun when itt ariseth in the high Heaven, so is the beauty of a good wife.'*

By the time Waller got back to Bath his troops of horse were but thin. Young Captain Edward Harley, for example, who had lost 10 horses and 2 men, charging the Cornish pikes, at Lansdown, had lost another 5 or 6 to Byron's swordsmen. Sir Arthur Hesilrige, hotly pursued by Richard Atkyns, owed his life to his pistol-proof armour. Cornet Robert Holmes – a future admiral – hit him but ' 'twas but a flea-biting him'. Atkyns pricked him in the neck. Captain Buck 'a very strong man, and charging with a mighty hanger [cutlass], stormed him and amazed him, but fell off again'. At length Sir Arthur said, 'What good will it do to you to kill a poor man?' He then took quarter, but whilst he was fumbling with his sword-knot, he was rescued by a runaway Roundhead troop. King Charles was told this story and made one of his few recorded jokes, commenting, 'Had he been victualled as well as fortified, he might have endured a siege of seven years.' . . . Not very good perhaps, but he was a serious-minded monarch.

Few battlefields are more worth a visit than that of Roundway Down. The broad sweep of Wiltshire downland carved by the Wansdyke, and the 'Bloody Ditch' below Oliver's Castle, where so many Roundheads broke their necks, have changed but little in three centuries. The castle, which is presumably Iron Age, has no more than an imaginary connection with Old Noll, who was

117

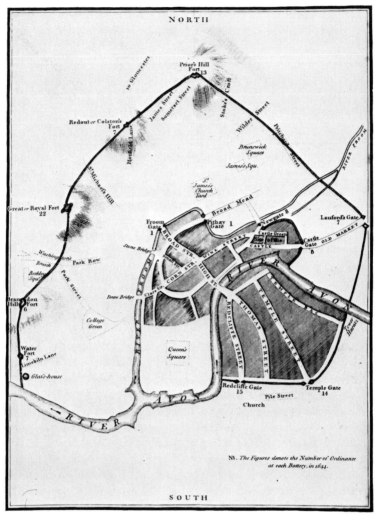

Sketch of the outworks of Bristol in 1644. (*Avon County Library Service*)

far away in East Anglia on the day when Wilmot brought relief to the Cornish Army on the downs above Devizes.

With Waller's army practically destroyed, the Royalist High Command rightly devined that their next move should be to capture Bristol, the second city of the kingdom, and a place where sympathy for the royal cause was by no means lacking. For this purpose the Western Army, now no more than 6,000 strong, was insufficient, and so the main role was allotted to

Prince Rupert with a strong contingent of the Oxford Army.

Bristol was held by Colonel Nathaniel Fiennes (*c*. 1608–69), whose portrait you may see at Broughton Castle near Banbury. He was the second son of William Fiennes, first Viscount Saye and Sele whose descendants still live at Broughton, which is open to the public.

Nathaniel Fiennes, who was MP for Banbury in the Long Parliament, had spoken forcefully in favour of the abolition of episcopacy. He had been involved in the rout at Powick Bridge (23 September 1642) but, according to Vicars' *Jehovah-Jireh* had been conspicuous for his courage. At Edgehill he had been in Sir William Balfour's Regiment, one of the two that broke through the Royalist centre. He had been acting as Governor of Bristol since February 1643, and had acted with decision, arresting his predecessor, Colonel Thomas Essex, for misconduct, and executing the Royalist plotters, George Bourchier and Robert Yeomans, who had attempted to open the gates to Prince Rupert (March).

It is clear from his correspondence that he had neither sufficient men to man his walls nor money enough to pay those he had. The line, vestiges of which may still be seen, was long and incomplete. Waller had drawn out 1,200 of the garrison, and lost them at Roundway Down. Even with modern infantry weapons his 3,000 men, half of them townsmen, would have been hard put to it to hold 4 miles of defences: with pike and musket it was well-nigh impossible. In addition to foot Fiennes had nearly 100 guns and some 300 horse.

119

Prince Rupert appeared on 23 July, making his reconnaissance from Durdham Down. The rocky ground was too difficult for digging approaches, and so the Cavaliers determined not to sap but to storm after a brief bombardment. Rupert was to attack on the north-west and Maurice with Hopton's Western Army on the south-west. The Cornish 'jumped the gun', and attacked at 3 a.m. on 26 July, before Rupert had given the signal. They attacked in three brigades:

Right   Colonel Brutus Buck
Centre   Colonel Sir Nicholas Slanning
Left   Major-General Thomas Bassett.

The men pushed carts and wagons forward, hoping to make bridges; but when they shoved them into the ditch it proved too deep. Prince Maurice, who had foreseen this, had provided his men with bundles of faggots and scaling ladders, and they fell on with their usual *élan*. Met with a heavy fire their losses were severe. They were compelled to fall back. Buck, Slanning and Trevanion were mortally wounded; Lieutenant-Colonel Barnard Astley and Bassett were wounded; Walter Slingsby helping to push a cart into the moat, fell in clad in his armour and was carried off unconscious. It may be that Hopton, had he been present, might have managed things better and spared his old army these tragic losses.

Rupert's men met with no better success at first. Lord Grandison whose brigade was repulsed from Stokes Croft and Prior's Hill Fort, was mortally wounded. Belasyse's tertia was foiled at Windmill Hill Fort. Then at last came the breakthrough. Wentworth's brigade, assaulting the line over rough ground between Brandon Hill and Windmill Hill forts, pushed down a re-entrant which they found sheltered them from the heavy flanking fire. Reaching the line they were in dead ground. They threw grenades over, and in the confusion that followed scrambled over the defences. The place was afterwards called 'Washington's Breach' for it was Colonel Henry Washington, great-uncle of the first President of the United States, that led the

The Royalists storm Bristol, 26 July 1643. 'Here, upon the steps (since called Lunsford's stairs), was the gallant Colonel [Henry] Lunsford shot through the heart, who had that day before been shot through the arm, . . .' The Journal of the Siege of Bristol. (*Avon County Library Service*)

way. Lieutenant-Colonel Edward Littleton (Bolle's Regiment) bravely rode round the inside of the line with a blazing fire-pike in his hand. Shouting 'Wildfire!' the defenders sprang down and fled towards the town.

Roundhead cavalry under Major Hercules Langrishe bore down on the breach, but not in time, for 300 Cavaliers were now within, with Royalist musketeers supporting them from the wall. Officers with fire-pikes rushed at the horses, which bolted off, wild-eyed and neighing.

With the line broken the fight was as good as won. The Cavaliers pushed on towards College Green, and the Quays. They stormed Frome Gate, despite the women of Bristol who were labouring to barricade with earth and woolsacks. In the fighting the brave Colonel Henry Lunsford fell, shot through the heart at a place known as Christmas Steps. The spot is marked by a plaque placed there by The Sealed Knot.

Fiennes now had really no alternative but surrender. Accused of treachery and cowardice he angrily demanded a trial, which took place at St Albans (14–23 December 1643). He was sentenced on the grounds of improper surrender. He owed his life to the good-natured old Earl of Essex. However, his military career was at an end.

Bristol was Rupert's greatest triumph. During the assault he had been everywhere, encouraging his men to prodigies of valour. Bristol with its wealth and its 30,000 inhabitants was to be a great asset to the Royalists in the next few years, until ironically enough, Rupert in turn was compelled to surrender the place to Sir Thomas Fairfax, and, like poor Fiennes, to find himself unjustly condemned by his own side.

The heavy losses among the senior officers made the Royalists very unwilling to attempt to take towns by storm, even when, as at Gloucester, there was a good chance that they would carry the day.

The old Cornish Army lived on under new leaders. John Grenvile commanded his father's old regiment; Slanning's passed to Bassett. But the old *joie de combattre* that had so distinguished it at Launceston, Stratton and at Lansdown, was blunted. The wheels of Charles ' wain were broken.

Mary Coate, the historian of the Civil War in Cornwall, has shown how greatly the Cornish had depended on these men:

' . . . the army which Grenvile and Hopton had led so triumphantly across the Tamar after Stratton had perished as surely as if it had fallen with Grenvile on the heights of Lansdown, or with Slanning by the walls of Bristol. For the life of the Cornish army had been in its leaders; they had inspired it with enthusiasm, they had given it its unity, and when they died its history ended. Lansdown and Bristol might be numbered among the Royalist triumphs, but for the Cornish army they were its Ichabod.'[1]

Note

1. *Cornwall in the Great Civil War and Interregnum*, 1642–1646, p. 100.

CHAPTER 8

Yorke Marche

If York be lost I shall esteem my crown little less; . . .
King Charles to Prince Rupert, 14 June 1644

Between 21 and 23 April 1644 the Earl of Leven and Lord Fairfax, laid siege to the city of York.

Leven had crossed the Border on 19 January with an army comprising:

Foot	18,000
Horse	2,000
Dragoons	1,000
	21,000

Wastage in the following three months had reduced the army to about 17,000.

Lord Fairfax commanded the Yorkshire Parliamentarian Army, some 5,000 strong.

The Marquis of Newcastle had gone north to oppose the Scots, and his men had fought delaying actions at Corbridge (18 February) and Hilton (23 March). But the defeat and capture of John Belasyse at Selby (11 April) led to a change of policy. Hearing of this disaster Newcastle had lost no time in adding the 4,000 infantry of his field army to the garrison of York (16 April). Most of the 3,000 cavalry, under Goring, he had sent away; the 800 retained were more than enough for the defenders in a siege.

On 6 May Manchester stormed Lincoln and on 3 June he brought the Army of the Eastern Association, which was in some ways the best of the Parliamentarian armies, to join the Allies before York.

York has been an important city since Roman times. There was

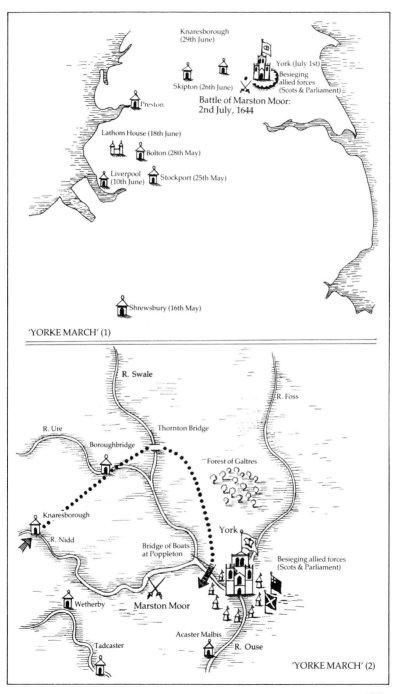

Knaresborough
(29th June)

Skipton (26th June)

York (July 1st)
Besieging
allied forces
(Scots & Parliament)

Battle of Marston Moor:
2nd July, 1644

Preston

Lathom House (18th June)

Bolton (28th May)

Liverpool
(10th June)

Stockport (25th May)

Shrewsbury (16th May)

'YORKE MARCH' (1)

R. Swale

R. Foss

R. Ure

Thornton Bridge

Boroughbridge

Forest of Galtres

Knaresborough

R. Nidd

York

Bridge of Boats
at Poppleton

Besieging allied forces
(Scots & Parliament)

Wetherby

Marston Moor

Tadcaster

Acaster Malbis

R. Ouse

'YORKE MARCH' (2)

a legionary fortress in the V formed by the confluence of the Rivers Foss and Ouse, and a civilian settlement in the present Micklegate area. In mediaeval times $3\frac{1}{2}$ miles of wall were built to enclose an area of some 260 acres. To a large extent they still exist. There was a quarter-mile gap between Layerthorpe Postern and the Red Tower, covered by the stagnant water of the King's Fishpond or Fishpool. This has now been drained, and the reclaimed land is known as Foss Islands. There was a keep, Clifford's Tower, where Colonel Sir Francis Cobbe of Ottringham was Governor.

There was a series of outer defence works, which protected the pastures outside the walls, where horses and cows could still safely be sent six weeks after the siege began.

York was a strong place, but its defences had been neglected during the years before the Civil War. Colonel-General Sir Thomas Glemham, a determined and experienced soldier, was Governor of York. He had seen to it that there were plentiful supplies for man and beast.

On 18 April Newcastle sent a decidedly gloomy letter to the King. Since Belasyse's defeat the Scots and Fairfax 'are now too strong for us in matters of the field . . . they have already put themselves in such a posture as will ruin us, being at York, unless there is some speedy course taken to give us relief, and that with a considerable force, for their army is very strong . . . We shall be distressed here very shortly.'

In fact the Parliamentarians did not invest the city very closely at first. One would think that, with some 22,000 men, they had sufficient troops for the purpose, but they were probably biding their time, waiting for the support of the Earl of Manchester.

On 13 May Lord Fairfax's men took a church, either St Nicholas' or St Lawrence's, which the Royalists were holding as an outpost. A company, eighty strong, was taken.

On 21 May a Scots officer, Lieutenant-Colonel Ballantine, was mortally wounded in a cavalry skirmish.

With the arrival of Manchester's army (3 June), at least 6,000 strong, the siege entered a more serious stage. Fairfax began to raise a battery on Lamel Hill (5 June). Leven stormed two of the three Royalist gun emplacements south-west of the city (8 June); and Fairfax's men began to try to mine Walmgate Bar (8 June). On the same day a 60 lb cannon-ball fired from Lamel Hill, went through the steeple of St Sampson's Church. In 1818 William Hargrove wrote that the 'perforation' made by this missile was still visible, but the church was badly damaged by fire in 1848, and in the rebuilding the marks of this shot vanished.

At this time the defenders were evidently anxious lest the enemy should get cover from the suburbs. On the morning of the 8th one of Newcastle's soldiers, in a red suit, was taken in Manchester's camp, he had with him pitch, flax and other materials 'for the fiering of the suburbs there, as yet free from the wasting flames'. On this same busy day: 'Divers Granadoes were cast from the Cittie into the Suburbs, when the Earle of Manchesters men were about fiering of the gate, to make passage into the Citie.'

Newcastle, playing for time, now wrote to Leven:

My Lord,
   I cannot but admire that your Lordship hath so neere beleaguered the Cittie on all sides, made batteries against it, and so neere approached to it, without signifying what your intentions are, and what you desire or expect, which is contrary to the rules of all military discipline and customes; therefore I have thought fit to remonstrate thus much to your Lordship, to the end that your Lordship may signifie your intentions and resolutions therein, and receive ours, and so I remain my Lord,
                    Your Lordships humble servant
                    Will[iam] Newcastle.
York 8, Iunii 1644
For his Excell[ency] the Earle of Levin [Leven].

This led to a considerable correspondence and on 14 June the three generals sent Newcastle 'Propositions', the first of which being 'that the Town shall be rendered within twenty dayes, in case no relief come to it by that time from the King or Prince Rupert, . . .'. The terms offered were good, but on the 15th Newcastle rejected them writing: 'I cannot suppose that your Lordshipps doe imagine that persons of honour can possibly condiscend to any of these propositions. . . .' By one of the oldest devices 'in the book', he had gained a week. The Marquis of Newcastle, so often dismissed as a mere grandee, was not lacking in cunning.

Meanwhile Prince Rupert had not been idle. He had set out from his HQ at Shrewsbury, upon what his *Journal* calls 'The Yorke Marche' on 16 May. His army comprised no more than 2,000 horse and 6,000 foot, but there were amongst them some

excellent regiments, which had been with the Prince in many of his successes, including, recently and notably, the relief of Newark. This was a period of the war when Rupert's was a name to conjure with. A Roundhead captain, whose account of Marston Moor is signed 'W.H.' calls him the Royalists' 'Goliath'. The Prince knew that he could not hope with 8,000 men, to break up the great and close siege of York.[1] He could hope, however, by moving into Lancashire to recruit his army. On 25 May he took Stockport, and on the 28th he stormed Bolton. The Earl of Derby was the first Cavalier to break in. The garrison was massacred: as many as 1,600 out of 2,500 are said to have been slain.

The young loyalists of a county that had been for a year under the power of the enemy poured in to join Rupert;
Lathom House was relieved, and on 30 May Goring and Sir Charles Lucas, with 5,000 horse and 800 foot belonging to Newcastle's army, as well as a great herd of cattle, rode in to swell the Prince's host. The Royalists now laid siege to Liverpool (7–11 June) and took it. The army, swollen to 14,000 men, was as ready as it would ever be to advance to the relief of York.

The King's thoughts, too, were, not unnaturally, upon his Northern Army. At Tickenhill on 14 June he took up his quill and, with the assistance of Lord Wilmot, concocted a letter which Rupert interpreted as a peremptory command to fight a battle with the armies besieging York, though how the letter can be given that construction is a mystery to me. The fact is that it was up to Rupert, as the man on the spot, to make up his own mind as to whether to offer battle or not (see Appendix A at end of the book).

Rupert left Preston on 23 June and marching by easy stages up the route of the present A59 via Clitheroe, and Gisburn, reached Skipton (36 miles from Preston) on the 26th, and rested so as to give his men time to 'fix their arms', whilst he sent messengers into York. Perhaps half his infantry were raw levies – one can imagine the company commanders putting them through the postures of the pike, during the summer evenings after the short day's march. 'Have a care! Advance – your – pikes! Port – your – pikes!' – and all that. The drill books of the day lay down endless movements for both musketeer and pikeman, yet pike-drill requires only about seven movements. A musketeer really only needs the orders: 'Make ready; take aim; give fire!'

York, 16 June 1644, Trinity Sunday

The treaty at an end the Allied commanders determined to storm, and next day, exploding a mine under St Mary's Tower, assaulted the manor.

> . . . This great house, originally the residence of the abbots of the monastery of St Mary, one of the richest Benedictine foundations in the north of England, had, after the Dissolution, become the headquarters and home of the Lord President of the Council of the North. Thomas Wentworth, Earl of Strafford, lived there from 1628 until 1633, when he went to Ireland. The Manor, Bootham Bar and the Minster constituted the strong points in the north-western defences of the city. St Mary's Tower, situated at an angle in the salient of the defences projecting into the lines of the Earl of Manchester, was an obvious point against which the besiegers might be expected to concentrate their attention.

The extensive grounds of the Manor, which included all the area now covered by the Museum Gardens, Yorkshire Museum, Art Gallery, York School of Art and Marygate Centre of Adult Education, had a garden, orchard and bowling green situated somewhere between St Mary's Tower and the Manor, all three of which played an important part in the day's events. (Wenham, p.57)

The plan was that, as soon as the three mines should be sprung, the Scots and Roundhead foot should 'go over the top'.

It is alleged that out of vanity Lieutenant-General Laurence Crawford sprang his mine too soon, hoping to win all the glory for Manchester's army. The Royalist, Colonel Sir Philip Byron,[2] who had the guard at St Mary's Tower, 'leading up some men was unfortunately kill'd as he open'd ye doors into ye bowling green whither ye enemy was gotten; but ye difficulty was not much, we soon beat ym out again . . .'.[3] In short, the assault was a disaster. Between 500 and 600 of Crawford's men entered the breach and at least 300 became casualties, 200–250 being taken prisoner. Simeon Ashe records the unpleasant aftermath.

'. . . On Munday morning (being the day following) some of our souldiers betwixt nine and ten a clock, approaching towards the place where the Tower stood, heard in the rubbish a very doleful cry, some calling, Help help; others, Water, water. Their lamentable complaints moved our men to resolve their relief; so they digged one out dead in the rubbish, & brought two alive; but from the Town such fierce opposition was made by the merciles[s] enemy against our Souldiers while they were labouring to save their friends lives, that they were compelled to leave many poore distressed ones dying in the dust.

Upon Wednesday or Thursday we obtained an hours time to bury our dead. . . .'

The successful defence by the Cavaliers cost them the lives of four brave officers: Colonel Sir Philip Byron; Colonel Huddleston; Lieutenant-Colonel Samuel Brearey and Captain Hackworth, an Irishman.

Skipton Castle. Prince Rupert rested his army here before his relief of York, 1644. (*Radio Times Hulton Picture Library*)

131

After this fiasco the Allies were very inactive during the rest of June. The besieged, however, made a sally against Manchester's leaguer. Some 600 men went out from Monk Bar, and were eventually driven back after suffering about 40 casualties.

By this time the Prince was drawing near and Newcastle tried to send messengers to inform him of the condition of the town. Sir Henry Slingsby, who lived at Red House at Nun Monkton, only 6 miles north-west of York wrote: '. . . They kept so strict guards, as I could not get any either in ye night, or day, to go to Red House & bring me back word how my children did, but were taken either going or coming.'

Signal fires were made upon the top of the Minster, and answered with similar signals from Pontefract Castle.

Prince Rupert, having made his final preparations, now moved forward once more and on 29 June slept at Sir Thomas Fairfax's house, Denton Hall in Wharfedale. He moved forward next day to Knaresborough, some of his cavalry appeared at Skip Bridge on the River Nidd, but 4 miles west of York. It seemed to the Allied commanders – doubtless as Rupert intended – that the Cavaliers meant to make a direct assault from the west.

The allies now raised their siege (29 June) and began to concentrate in and around Hessay, Long Marston and Tockwith, Manchester's men crossing the Ouse by a bridge of boats at Poppleton, and Fairfax's by one in the Fulford/Middlethorpe area.

Rupert now executed a very skilful manœuvre. The three

St Mary's Tower, York. Damage from the mine exploded prior to the assault on 16 June 1644 may be seen. (*National Monuments Record – Crown Copyright reserved*)

Allied armies were concentrated on Marston Moor, 6 miles west of York on the Knaresborough road. The Prince amused them by showing them an advanced guard of cavalry, and the enemy riposted by drawing up their men in battle array, ready to receive the main body of the Royalist Army. But the hours ticked by and no Royalist Army appeared. Crossing the Ure at Boroughbridge, 7 miles north-east of Knaresborough, the Prince had pushed on passing the Swale at Thornton Bridge. Then wheeling round to the South-east he made for York down the north bank of the Ouse, and surprised the Roundhead dragoons guarding Manchester's bridge of boats at Poppleton. Rupert's swift encircling movement of 20 miles completely deceived his opponents. By nightfall York had been relieved. The Allies, outmanœuvred, decided to withdraw south-west, making for Tadcaster. They expected a reinforcement under Meldrum.

The Royalists, too, expected some 2,000 men under Sir Robert Clavering. Newcastle, very reasonably, wished to await them, and to give his men some rest after the toil and peril of the siege. But the Prince, with that damned letter in his pocket, was bent on battle, and, having just demonstrated his very considerable tactical skill, was not taking no for an answer, whatever the courtly Marquis, or his canny chief of staff, James King, Lord Eythin, might say to the contrary.

It would have been simple enough for Rupert to keep his army east of the Ouse, where he could await Clavering in security, while he melded Newcastle's army with his own.

In all probability the three Allied armies would now have gone their several ways had not the Prince practically compelled them to fight him. As the odds against him, in numbers, were something like three to two it was hardly prudent.

The battle that followed was not complicated.

The army was arrayed much as you see it in the map, the troops taking up their positions as they arrived. Newcastle's Foot under Mackworth came on the scene rather late, for they had been drinking and pillaging the abandoned Allied camp.

There was a flurry of gunfire during the afternoon, which killed a Lancastrian Royalist, Captain Roger Houghton. Then things fell quiet and it began to look as if there would be no fight until the 3rd Lord Eythin criticized Rupert's dispositions, telling him very rudely: 'By God, Sir, it is very fine in the paper, but there is no such thing in the field.'

Towards evening the Allied generals, sitting their horses, it

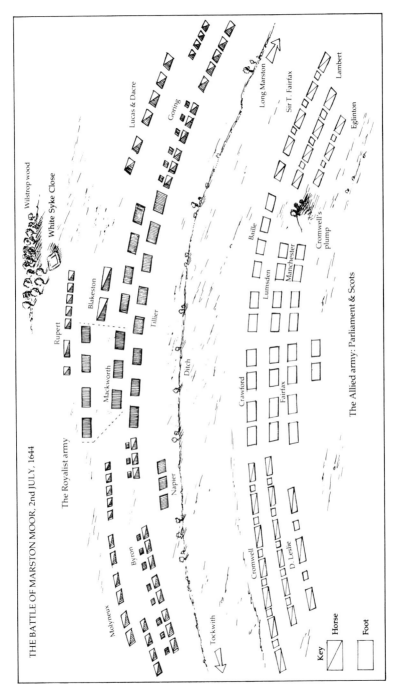

THE BATTLE OF MARSTON MOOR, 2nd JULY, 1644

The Royalist army

Wilstrop wood

White Syke Close

Rupert

Blakeston

Mackworth

Tillier

Molyneux

Byron

Napier

Tockwith

Ditch

Lucas & Dacre

Goring

Long Marston

Sir T. Fairfax

Lambert

Eglinton

Baille

Lumsden

Manchester

Cromwell's plump

Crawford

Fairfax

Cromwell

D. Leslie

The Allied army: Parliament & Scots

Key

Horse

Foot

may be, near Cromwell's Plump, detected the smoke of campfires ascending to heaven. The Royalists were preparing their supper: this was the moment to fall on. And so they did, moving swiftly down the hillside in a 'running march'. On the Allied right Sir Thomas Fairfax met with a rough reception from Goring, Lucas, Langdale, Dacre, Carnaby and a host of rugged northern horse. His men scattered to the four winds. Sir Thomas, his cheek slashed open, tore off his field-sign and made his way through the great bodies of Royalist horse and foot, passing for a Cavalier.

The foot in the centre made some progress, but were then held.

Cromwell, however, at the head of his famous Ironsides did well against Lord Byron. The latter, despite Rupert's direct order to stay north of the ditch came across it to meet Oliver. It may be that he wanted to get up speed before the clash, but stupid, dogged Byron is somewhat suspect as a tactician, and it may be that he would have done better to stick to the letter of his orders.

During the first phase of the battle, Colonel Marcus Trevor (later Lord Dungannon) mounted perhaps on his jewel, Bay Squire, who was lost that autumn at Montgomery Castle, sought out and wounded Cromwell. This was tradition in his family, and is not in the least unlikely seeing that Trevor and Cromwell were posted more or less opposite one another. Certainly Oliver was compelled to quit the field for a space, riding to Tockwith to have his wound dressed.

In the second phase Goring endeavoured to exploit his success; Lucas, his second-in-command charged the right wing of the Scots foot, doubtless relieving the pressure on Tillier's Greencoats.

The valiant Sir William Blackiston led his brigade of horse in a charge which broke into Lumsden's foot, wreaking havoc.

Rupert led a countercharge against the cavalry of Cromwell and David Leslie, and on the authority of Watson, the Ironsides' Scoutmaster, 'Cromwell's own division had a hard pull of it; for they were charged by Rupert's bravest men both in front and flank; they stood at the sword's point a pretty while, hacking one another, but at last (it so pleased God) he brake through them, scattering them before him like a little dust.' Lord Saye, too, attests the severity of the fighting with Rupert's Horse, who 'being many of them, if not the greatest part, gentlemen, stood very firm a long while, coming to a close fight with the sword, and standing like an iron wall, so that they were not easily

A
DOGS ELEGY, <u>17</u>
OR
RVPERT'S TEARS,

For the late Defeat given him at *Marston-moore*, neer *York*, by the Three Renowned
Generalls; *Alexander Earl of* Leven, *Generall of the Scottish Forces,* Fardinando *Lord* Fairefax, *and the Earle of* Man-chefter *Generalls of the* English *Forces in the North.*

Where his beloved Dog, named *B O Y*, was killed by a Val-liant Souldier, who had skill in *Necromancy.*

Likewise the ftrange breed of this Shagg'd Cavalier, *whelp'd of a Malignant* Water-witch; *With all his Tricks, and Feats.*

Sad Cavaliers, *Rupert* invites you all   } Clofe-mourners are the Witch, Pope, & devill,
That doe furvive, to his Dogs Funerall. } That much lament yo'r late befallen evill.

Printed at *London,* for *G. B.* July 27. 1644.

A casualty of Marston Moor. Boy was in fact a large white poodle. (*Mansell Collection*)

broken; . . .'. By this time many of the generals had fled the field.

The last phase of the battle began with a series of counter-attacks by the Allies. Though Fairfax's Horse had vanished, some of the foot held out, clumps of pikes standing, rock-like in a swirling sea of Cavalier horse. David Leslie with his three regiments of Scots horse, which acted as a reserve to Cromwell, tipped the balance against Rupert, who was compelled to take cover in a beanfield, and so lost control of the battle. Many of his men, seeking safety, galloped away round Wilstrop Wood, and in his haste one of them knocked over and killed a luckless country girl, who was holding a gate open for the runaways.

Cromwell and Leslie now moved round the rear of the Royalist foot and sought out Goring..The latter's cavalry was by this time in grave disorder, and soon the survivors were making what speed they could to York, though some like the formidable Langdale did not leave the field until midnight.

The last episode of this strange battle, much of it fought in the dark, was the destruction of Newcastle's Whitecoats, who scorning surrender, fought to the bitter end in White Syke Close.

At Marston Moor Rupert lost the North. It was to prove an irretrievable disaster. Newcastle took ship for Hamburg, and thereafter nothing remained of his great army save two small brigades of horse under Langdale and Blackiston, and half a dozen resolute garrisons.

Rupert withdrew by the way he had come, leaving York to its fate. Whether he considered hovering about Skipton Castle, whence he might perhaps have raided the Allies' rear, cannot be said. It might not have been a bad idea. Evidently the Prince thought his army too shattered to make any further effort to save the besieged city.

And thus York *was* lost, and so in the long run was King Charles' crown, but the King lost that for himself at Naseby.

Notes

1.' . . . The very best Harmonical-Musick that ever I heard . . . was in the year 1644 . . . in the stately Cathedral of the Loyal City York. . . . The occasion of it was, the great and close Siege . . . strictly maintain'd for eleven weeks space, by three very notable and considerable great Armies.' Thomas Mace, in *Musick's Monument*, 1676.

2. One of the five loyal brothers of John, Lord Byron.

3. Slingsby, p.109 (*see bibliography for Ch.2*).

CHAPTER 9

The offensive of the New Model Army

Finis coronat opus[1]

When in April 1645 Sir Thomas Fairfax took the field with the New Model Army the Parliament had already gained the upper hand for, at the great battle of Marston Moor, Prince Rupert had lost the North for the King.

In Scotland Montrose still kept the Royalist cause alive, but in England north of the Trent only eight important garrisons remained to the King and all of them were, if not besieged, at least blockaded.

Cumberland

	Governor	Surrendered
Carlisle	Colonel-General Sir Thomas Glemham, Bart. Colonel Sir Philip Musgrave, Bart.	2 or 25 July 1645

Lancashire

Lathom House Greenhaugh Castle	Colonel Edward Rosthern	2 December 1645

Yorkshire

Scarborough Castle	Colonel Sir Hugh Cholmley	22 July 1645
Pontefract Castle	Colonel Sir John Redman	21 July 1645
Sandal Castle	Captain George Bonivant	2 October 1645
Bolton Castle	Colonel John Scrope	November 1645
Skipton Castle	Colonel Sir John Mallory, Bart.	21 December 1645

OFFENSIVE OF THE NEW MODEL ARMY
1645

Key
🏠 Towns & cities
⚙ Sieges
✖ Scots
♞ Royalists
🏰 Parliament

THE NASEBY CAMPAIGN
←——— The King
-◄- - - Fairfax

Newcastle

York

Pontefract

Newark

Chester

Shrewsbury

Leicester

Market Harborough

NASEBY

Worcester
Evesham

Northampton

Daventry

Gloucester

Stow

Oxford

Bristol

Reading

London

Newbury

Langport

Taunton

Blandford

Plymouth

Weymouth

South of the Trent the Parliament controlled a solid block of territory comprising London, Rutland, Huntingdonshire, Cambridgeshire, Norfolk, Suffolk, Essex, Bedfordshire, Hertfordshire, Middlesex, Surrey, Kent and Sussex. This was the most populous, and economically well developed part of the kingdom; an area, not altogether lacking in Cavaliers, but one from which Charles could in fact draw very little support.

In the Midlands and Wales, which were still disputed, the strength of the two sides was more evenly balanced. The Royalists had complete control of Herefordshire, and all of Worcestershire save the relatively unimportant garrison of Hawksley House. In Shropshire the Roundheads held Shrewsbury, Wem and Oswestry, but the Cavaliers had a dozen strongholds, the most important being Ludlow and Bridgnorth.

The Roundheads held Stafford, but the Royalists with Lichfield and Dudley Castle in their hands disputed control of the county, though there was ill-feeling between their governors, Colonel Richard Bagot and Thomas Leveson.

In Cheshire the Roundhead, Sir William Brereton, had Nantwich for his base, but Lord Byron had a strong garrison in Chester, and a ring of castles round about.

In Leicestershire the Royalist leader, Lord Loughborough, known to the enemy as Rob-Carrier, with his HQ at Ashby de la Zouch kept a watchful eye on Leicester town.

Lincolnshire, though largely Royalist in sympathy, was entirely in Roundhead hands.

In Nottinghamshire the county town was balanced by Newark and its ring of satellite fortresses, a Royalist stronghold of very real importance.

In Wales the Parliament had garrisons in Pembroke and at Montgomery Castle, but most of the Principality was still held for the King, who had garrisons at Raglan Castle, Monmouth, Chepstow, Flint Castle, Holt Castle, Denbigh, Aberystwyth, Conway, Carmarthen, Caernarvon and Harlech Castle.

The Royalists' main strength lay around their capital, Oxford, and in the South west.

In Devon and Cornwall only Plymouth, which was blockaded or besieged practically throughout the war, held out for the Parliament. The Cavaliers had many garrisons, large and small, the most important being, perhaps, Falmouth, Exeter, Barnstaple and Dartmouth.

In Somerset only Taunton held out for the Parliament:

Bristol, Bridgwater and Bath were all in Royalist hands.

In Dorset the Parliament was in the ascendant, holding the ports of Lyme, Weymouth and Poole. The Cavaliers had nothing but the three castles of Portland, Corfe and Sherborne.

In the broad plain of Wiltshire neither side was really strong. The Roundheads of Malmesbury, were perhaps somewhat outnumbered by the garrisons of Devizes, Lacock House, Longford House and Highworth.

The Parliament held the Hampshire coast with Portsmouth, Southampton and Christchurch in its power; but inland Winchester and Basing House still held out for the King.

In Oxfordshire, Berkshire and Buckinghamshire the Royalists had their headquarters and its protective circle of satellite fortresses: Banbury, Woodstock, Gaunt House, Bletchingdon House and Godstow (Oxfordshire). In Berkshire they held three castles: Donnington, Faringdon and Wallingford, but the Roundheads had held Windsor from the outset; Reading since April, and Abingdon since June 1644; the capture of the last named piercing the outer circle of Oxford's defences.

In Buckinghamshire the Cavaliers had only Boarstall House, blocking an exit from Otmoor, which was as yet undrained, and so protected Oxford from the north-east. The Parliamentarians held Aylesbury.

This account of the garrisons is by no means exhaustive. Both sides locked up thousands of men in fortresses, some of which were of very doubtful value.

The battle of Naseby, fought between the New Model and the King's main, or 'Oxford' Army, transformed the strategy of the war. Sir Thomas Fairfax's victory won him a measure of independence. The Committee of Both Kingdoms, sitting at Derby House, London, no longer felt that it behoved it to dictate every move he made.

In Fairfax's place a modern strategist would now perhaps have considered two alternatives.

1. Lay siege to Oxford and capture the Royalist capital and headquarters.
2. Seek out and destroy the Royalist Army under Goring in the West Country.

Sir Thomas chose neither course. His first move, sensibly enough was to retake Leicester, which the Cavaliers had as yet not had time to put in a state of defence (18 June). This done, Fairfax decided to invade Somerset, where after taking the minor garrison of Highworth, Wiltshire (27 June), he appeared early in July. Taunton was now relieved for the second time (3 July), and Colonel Robert Phelips of Montacute was compelled to quit Ilchester garrison (8 July). This led to the New Model's second pitched battle: Langport, fought near the market town of that name, on the right (east) bank of the River Parret, and near the village of Huish Episcopi with its beautiful Perpendicular church tower. Goring had evidently lost his nerve by this time. He decided that he was beaten even before he was attacked, and on 9 July sent his baggage and all but two of his guns to Bridgwater, thus virtually abandoning the line of the Parret.

Langport was in one way an unusual battle in that the Parliamentarian artillery was for once used to good effect. The 'Ordnance were drawn down to places of advantage' and 'began to play (a good while before the foot engaged) doing great execution upon the body of the enemies Army, both horse and foot, who stood in good order upon the hill, (about musket shot from the passe)[2] and forcing them to draw off their Ordnance, and their horse to remove their ground'.

This done, the New Model foot advanced from hedge to hedge until they got the pass. The Cavaliers rode down to countercharge, but were foiled by Major Christopher Bethell[3] of Whalley's Regiment, who with the Forlorn Hope of the Parliamentarian horse made a brave charge, and broke the body he fought with, and its supports. Then Major John Desbrowe of Fairfax's Regiment, 'the grym gyant Disbrowe' as he was called, came up with the reserve and 'charged the next standing bodies of the enemy so home, that instantly they put them to a disorderly retreat'. (Sprigg, p. 65). Roundhead musketeers came up to support the horse, 'firing upon the enemy, whereupon their Regiments of white Colours, and black Colours of foot, before ever they engaged, marched away apace; . . .'. History does not record whose these two cautious Royalist regiments were.

The Cavaliers fled about 2 miles and then made a stand 'in plaine green field (where the passage out was narrow) called *Aller Drove* but received only a piece of a charge, and then seeing our bodies coming on orderly and fast, faced about, and never stood after'. (Sprigg, p. 66). The New Model pursued the Cavaliers for 8 miles taking 1,400 prisoners and some 30 colours and 2 guns. The departing Royalists quit Langport garrison, setting fire to the place as they went, 'but by the industry of the soldiers and Townesmen it was quenched'.

Neither Goring nor his army had shown much resolution in this action, nor is that altogether strange for they may well have expected that Charles, having no other field army, would put himself at their head. The addition of the horse which Rupert and Langdale had led at Naseby, and Charles Gerard's small army from South Wales would have enabled the Western Cavaliers to make head against the New Model. But at this juncture the King was strangely inactive. It was as if he went on leave!

Fairfax was now in a position to mop up the remaining Cavalier strongholds in Somersetshire and this, before the end of August, he had done with the single exception of Dunster Castle.

		Garrison	Guns	
13 July	Burrough Hill Fort	160	–	Yielded
23 July	Bridgwater	1,600	44	Stormed
30 July	Bath	140	6	Yielded
20 August	Nunney Castle	...	..	Yielded
28 August	Portishead Point Fort	...	6	Yielded

Dunster fell in April 1646, after a siege of 150 days.

At Bridgwater the Cavaliers under Colonel Sir Hugh Wyndham, put up a stiff resistance, holding out against two attempts to storm. They refused a treaty after part of the town was taken, fired the part the Roundheads were in 'and rang the bells for joy when they saw it blaze . . .'. Lady Wyndham is also said to have taken a pot-shot at Cromwell with a musket, and to have sent him a message asking how he liked 'her love token'.

In August Fairfax besieged and took what Sprigg calls the impregnable castle of Sherborne, where Colonel Sir Lewis Dyve, 'an active Enemy, and resolute Souldier . . .', put up a stiff resistance for sixteen days. The place, which had already been besieged in 1642, is well worth a visit.

Dyve had a garrison of some 400 with 18 guns and a mortar. His men included several gamekeepers, who picked off a number of Roundhead officers and gunners. Fairfax brought up miners from the Mendips, and as the stone upon which the castle was built is soft they managed to mine it without undue difficulty. This is a brief diary of the siege:

27 July: Reconnaissance by Colonel Pickering and a brigade of New Model horse and foot.

1 August: Reconnaissance by Fairfax.

2 August: Reconnaissance by Fairfax and Cromwell.

5 August: A 'commanded party' gains the haystack within a stone's cast of the Royalist works. Dyve sets his men to build new works for ordnance.

6 August: Dyve rejects Fairfax's second summons.

Fairfax holds a council of war and decides to reduce the castle by approaches, mining and batteries.

A Royalist marksman with a birding piece shoots Captain Horsey [Thomas Rainsborough's Foot] from one of the towers.

7 August: Captain Horsey and Captain-Lieutenant Fleming buried 'after a martiall manner' in the church at Sherborne, the place where his 'Ancestors were intombed' (Sprigg, p. 71).

8 August: Fairfax, going to visit the mine, was nearly shot by some of his men who 'encompassing some Dear round' killed one of their fellows! 'Very freely did the souldiers work in the Mines and Galleries and making of Batteries, every man being rewarded twelve pence a piece for the day, and as much for the night, for the service was hot and hazardous' (Sprigg, p.83).

By this time Dyve's marksmen had mortally wounded Major John Done, and his successor, Thomas Crosse, and shot Captain Thomas (?) Creamer.

11 August: Cannon, pay and Mendip miners arrived. Dyve's men 'Threw Fiery Faggots over those parts of the Wall where the Miners were . . .' (Sprigg, p. 83).

Fairfax was short of ammunition and paid 6*d.* apiece for every cannon-ball his soldiers retrieved from under the castle walls! Still, confident of success he sent to Dyve that if he pleased to send out his lady, or any other women, he would permit it. 'Sir Lewis thankfully acknowledged the favour, seemed to incline to accept of it, but gave no positive answer, expressing withall his resolution (souldier-like) to hold out to the last.' To Sprigg this seemed 'a madnesse rather then valour, seeing he despaired of relief' (Sprigg, p. 83).

13 August: The Roundheads brought their heavy battering pieces into position, and Dyve's marksmen picked off two of their gunners.

14 August: 11 a.m.–6 p.m. The great guns made a breach in the middle wall, wide enough for ten men to march abreast and beat down one of the towers. Fairfax sent in a third summons, and Dyve, who alleged, in a passion, that the drummer was

Sherborne Castle. It was stormed by Sir Thomas Fairfax after an eleven days' seige on 15 August 1645. (*Crown Copyright – reproduced with the permission of the Controller of Her Majesty's Stationery Office*)

saucy – said he would not lose his honour to save his life.

The Roundheads managed to seize a tower in the corner of the castle, from which they picked off one of Dyve's chief marksmen.

15 August: Dyve offered to surrender to which Fairfax, having possession of the breach and some of the towers, replied, albeit courteously, that he was obliged in honour 'to agree to no other Conditions than Quarter for your lives; . . .'.

Dyve had now no alternative but to surrender, for his disheartened men were crying out for quarter.

The Roundhead soldiers, who wanted booty rather than revenge, plundered their 400 prisoners most thoroughly, though Dyve, his lady and a few others were spared this treatment. The chief prisoners were Dyve's uncle, Sir John Walcot, his brother-in-law, Colonel Sir Giles Strangways, MP, and Colonel Richard Thornhill. The spoils included 16 guns, a mortar, a 'murderer', 600 arms and 39 barrels of powder, besides plentiful provisions.

Fairfax's messenger, Walter Curtis, received a gift of £20 from the House of Commons, and on the 22nd Members attended a service of thanksgiving at St Margaret's, Westminster, for the taking of Sherborne, Bridgwater, Bath, Cannon Froome and Scarborough, listening to edifying and doubtless lengthy sermons from Mr Case and Mr John Bond, Minister of the Savoy. The latter described Sherborne in the language of the fanatic: '. . . O that first Westerne nest of the Cockatrice's egges, the cradle of Cavalierisme, the very bugge of the Westerne Imposthume. . . .'

Mercurius Britannicus, though an enemy, had a generous word to say of Dyve: 'What pitty 'tis that Gallant men should have no better a Cause to suffer for!'

The prisoners were shipped by sea to London. Before being taken to the Tower Sir Lewis was brought before the House of Commons. 'He kneeling in a sleight and careless posture but upon one knee at the Bar was commanded to kneele on both, whereupon he seemed to give a smiling and deriding countenance.'

After two years in the Tower, Dyve was removed to the King's Bench because of his debts. Thence he made his escape in January 1648.

Sherborne, with only 19 guns and some 400 men had held out for 11 days. It may be that the men would have been more useful had they served with the main army at Naseby, but, it must be

considered that the garrison encouraged the local Clubmen, who seem to have been anti-Parliament as well as anti-war, besides controlling a large tract of territory in North Dorset.

Fairfax now turned against Bristol, where Rupert with 3,000 men, or more, only held out for 18 days before it was stormed. The plague was sore in the city, and the villages about it, and 100 were dying each week. But it was 'the only considerable Port the King had in the whole Kingdom, for shipping, and trade, and riches; being withall his magazine for all sort of Ammunition: . . .' (Sprigg, p. 88). So on the whole the New Model's Council of War thought it best to take Bristol before moving against Goring in the South-west. Captain Moulton, Admiral for the Irish Coasts, was ordered to blockade Bristol by sea.

The siege began badly for the Prince for on 23 August the Captain of his Lifeguard, Sir Richard Crane, who had been with him throughout the war, sallied out with a party of horse and was mortally wounded. On the 26th Sir Barnard Astley, who had commanded a tertia at Naseby, met a similar fate.

On 31 August the Roundheads intercepted a letter of the 25th, in which Goring at Exeter assured Secretary Nicholas that in three weeks' time (say, by 15 September) he would be ready to interrupt Fairfax in his siege before Bristol. Of course, no such thing came to pass . . . nor did Rupert hold out so long. On 10 September after various propositions for surrender the New Model stormed the line. The signal for the general assault was the firing of a great heap of straw and faggots on the top of a hill, and a salvo from four great guns against Prior's Hill Fort. Then 'immediately the storm began round the City, and was terrible to the beholder' (Sprigg, p. 106).

Colonels Edward Montagu and John Pickering speedily broke in at Lawford's Gate, taking twenty-two great guns and many prisoners. Lieutenant-Colonel Thomas Jackson with the regiments of Fairfax and Sir Hardress Waller entered between Lawford's Gate and the River Frome. Colonels Thomas Rainsborough and Robert Hammond broke in near Prior's Hill Fort. Skippon's and Colonel John Birch's regiments got in nearer the Frome. Pioneers came forward to make gaps in the line, and in went the cavalry.

Prior's Hill held out for two hours, and, refusing quarter, Major Price and most of his garrison were massacred. Some four hours later the Prince sent a trumpeter to desire a parley, and by 7 o'clock that night articles had been concluded. It is easy to say that Rupert could have hung on to the castle, but the fact is that the line was too long for the men available. He marched out with every mark of respect from Fairfax and the New Model. His enemies were of his own side. Lord Digby now managed to stab him in the back, and easily persuaded his fickle uncle to deprive him of his command.

The spoils of Bristol were considerable. About 100 guns, with 100 barrels of powder, and other ammunition in proportion; something like 2,500 muskets. The Royal Fort was victualled for 150 men for 320 days; the castle for 160 days. The garrison is said to have comprised:

```
    1,000  horse
    2,500  foot
1,000–1,500  townsmen
4,500–5,000
```

Neither the King nor Goring made any attempt to relieve Bristol. The Prince, thus left to his own devices, might conceivably have done better, but it is difficult to see what else he could do but to try to defend a line, which with the weapons of those days, required a far stronger garrison.

More mopping-up followed, in Wiltshire, Gloucestershire and Hampshire.

23 September:	Devizes Castle, Wilts.	Yielded
24 September:	Lacock House, Wilts.	Yielded
25 September:	Berkeley Castle, Glos.	Stormed
8 October:	Winchester Castle, Hants.	Yielded
14 October:	Basing House, Hants.	Stormed
18 October:	Longford House, Wilts.	Yielded

I cannot pretend to have visited all these places, but Lacock, and Basing are both worth a visit, whilst Berkeley Castle, scene of the strange demise of that peculiar monarch, King Edward II, is particularly worth a visit. In the Civil Wars it was a satellite fortress to the Royalist garrison of Bristol, 24 miles to the south. One Forbes, quite the place when Rupert took the city. Then Captain, later Major, George Maxwell, a Scot, commissioned by the Prince, was put in there with 320 foot (29 August 1643). By 9 September 1644 Colonel Thomas Veale (*c*. 1591–1663) was Governor. Next came Colonel Richard Poore, who was killed near Lydney in the Forest of Dean on 22 February 1645, and buried in Chepstow Church three days later. He was followed, or replaced by Sir Charles Lucas, one of Rupert's band of swordsmen, an excellent cavalry general, who would have been better employed as the commander of a cavalry brigade rather than the governor of a fortress. He had a garrison of 500 horse and foot with 11 guns. One of Lucas' officers told a Roundhead captain of horse, 'He thought God was turned Roundhead, the King's forces prospered so ill' (Sprigg, p. 126).

Sprigg, who describes all these sieges, tells us that Devizes was 'a place of great strength, having been an old fortification, raised on a huge Mount of earth' (p. 122). Its Governor, Colonel Sir Charles Lloyd, an experienced engineer 'had added to the strength of its naturall scituation, what Art could do, having cut out of the main Earth severall Works commanding one another, and so strong that no Canon could pierce them; besides, that being pallizadoed, and stockaded in most places, it was a matter of extream difficulty to storm it' (pp. 122 and 123). The palisades and stockades took the place of the barbed wire and anti-personnel mines used in our own days.

Summoned to surrender Lloyd replied, '*Win it and weare it*', but mortar fire solved the Roundheads' problem. 'some of the Granadoes breaking in the midst of the castle (being open above) kill'd severall of their men, and much endangered the blowing up of the Magazine; which so startled the Enemy that they sounded a parley' (Sprigg, p. 123). The garrison was 400 strong, but had, it seems only two pieces of ordnance.

At Winchester Cromwell gave Lord Ogle good terms, for he timed his surrender rather more prudently than Dyve had done at Sherborne. The garrison of the castle was 700 with 7 guns and Cromwell thought 'the Works were exceeding good and strong . . .'. The place was well victualled. The list of ammunition and provisions taken is interesting as showing what a diligent governor tried to procure before standing a siege:

7 pieces of ordnance
17 barrels of powder
20 cwt of musket bullets
8 cwt of match
38 hogsheads of beef and pork
150 lbs of cheese
800 lbs of butter
140 quarters of wheat and meal
3 hogsheads of French wine
10 quarters of salt
20 bushels of oatmeal
70 dozen candles
30 load of wood
40 quarters of charcoal
30 bushels of sea-coal
14 sheep
4 quarters of fresh beef
70 cwt of biscuits
112 hogsheads of strong beer.

Contrary to the articles, six Roundhead troopers plundered some of the garrison when they marched out. They were apprehended, tried by court martial and condemned to die. They cast lots for their lives and one suffered death. The other five were handed over to Sir Thomas Glemham, the Royalist Governor of Oxford, to be put to death, or otherwise punished as he should think fit. Glemham, impressed by Cromwell's desire to see right done, returned them with an acknowledgement of his 'Noblenesse, in being so tender in breach of articles' (Sprigg, p. 133). Such were the military manners of our ancestors.

But they could be rough enough when they chose as Cromwell's next siege, Basing House, demonstrates. The garrison, being Roman Catholics, were particularly obnoxious to the Roundheads, and in the storm seventy-four were slain, including the daughter of Doctor Griffith, 'who by her railing provoked our Souldiers (then in heat) into a further passion'. Major Thomas Harrison (of Charles Fleetwood's Regiment of Horse) is said to have killed Major John Cufaud and Major Robinson as they were getting over the works. The Royalists later spread the story that he had shot Robinson in cold blood after he had laid down his arms, saying, 'Cursèd is he that doeth the work of the Lord negligently.' However, Harrison the regicide, for all his faults was a man of exceptional courage and the story does not seem to be altogether in character.

The Governor of Basing was a Catholic, John Paulet, fifth Marquis of Winchester (1598–1675) the great loyalist, who, with his house blazing around him, told Hugh Peters, the Roundhead chaplain, *That if the King had no more ground in England but Bazing-house, he would adventure as he did and, so maintain it to his uttermost*. Not for nothing had he taken AIMEZ LOYAUTÉ for his motto. It fell to Mr Peters' lot to present the Marquis' captured standard to the Commons. It bore the motto DONEC PAX REDDIT TERRIS.

The end of October found Fairfax in Devonshire, where Tiverton Castle was stormed on 20 October. The New Model was 'much wearied out with the extreme wet weather, and their carriages broken' (Sprigg, p. 147). It was in a very sickly state by this time, Colonel John Pickering 'that pious, active Gentleman, that lived so much to God, and his country', being one of those who succumbed to 'the new disease.' The New Model's conquering progress was quite halted. Steps were taken to straiten Exeter but it was not until January 1646 that there was any more serious fighting.

Cromwell surprised the bibulous Lord Wentworth at Bovey Tracey on 9 January, taking 60 prisoners, 400 horse, and 7 colours, one of which bore a crown and C.R. upon it. It was almost supper-time when the Parliamentarians entered the town, and most of the Cavaliers were playing cards. Many of the principal officers were together in one room. They threw the stakes out of the window and whilst the Roundhead troopers

Overleaf: Berkeley Castle. A Civil War outpost of the Royalist garrison of Bristol.

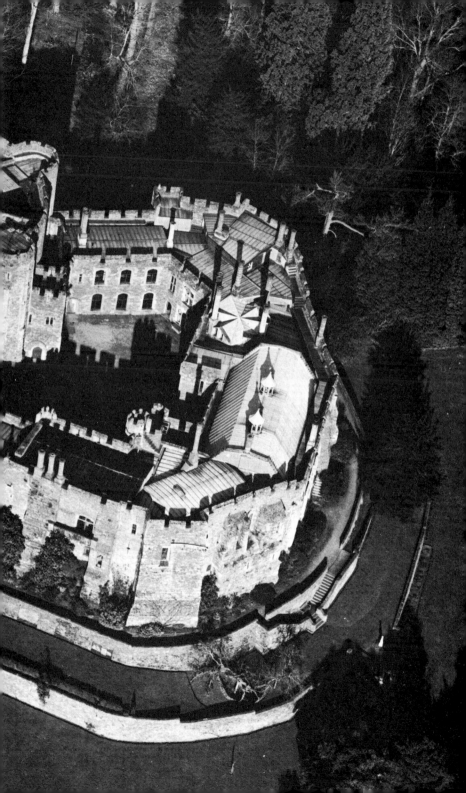

were scrambling for them, the Cavalier commanders escaped out at a back door and over the river! A week later Fairfax relieved Plymouth, compelling the Royalists to quit their forts, undemolished, and abandon seven guns (16 January). Three days later in very mild weather, following a hard frost, the New Model stormed Dartmouth, taking Mount Boone, the West Gate, Tunstal Church and the town itself, with more than sixty guns. Two men-of-war lying in the river surrendered. This exploit cost the Roundheads but one man killed and very few wounded, which does not say much for the defence.

Sir Henry Cary, whose regiment, with twelve guns, held Kingsworth (Kingswear?) Fort, made conditions and marched out with his officers and men. The rest of the garrison, about 1,000, became prisoners. Fairfax released such as were Cornishmen, with 2s. a man to get them home. 'That the Cornish might see, we had forgot former injuries, and respected them as much as any other County' (Sprigg, p. 171).

Powderham Castle yielded a week later (25 January).

February is a good month to spend in winter quarters, but in the middle of it Lord Hopton, who now commanded what remained of the Western Army took the field in a last forlorn attempt to relieve Sir John Berkeley in Exeter. His banner bore the strange device 'I will strive to serve my soveraigne King', which somehow leaves one wondering whether he had much hope that his expedition would succeed.

Estimates of his strength vary:

	Hopton	Sprigg
Horse	3,300	5,000
Foot	1,890	4,000
	5,190	9,000

The lower figure is certainly the correct one, for Hopton, besides being the person best placed to know, was an honest and intelligent witness. The discipline of most of his horse had deteriorated to the extent that as he put it: 'We were never able to surprise, or attempt upon the enemy, but ever liable to be surprised by them.' From these strictures we must except Prince Charles' 'Regiment of Horse, which had been remodelled the previous autumn. The Cornish Trained Bands were also 'full of complaints and all sorts of distempers', but as Hopton had only 150 of them with him that was not so serious.

Hopton advanced from Stratton to Torrington, 18 miles, in one day, which was good by the standards of the mid-seventeenth century. On the 14th Hopton learned that Fairfax was approaching, and threw up barricades of earth at the various entrances to Torrington. Major-General William Webb with 200 men rode out a mile to Stevenstone Park, to reconnoitre the approaching enemy, but was driven back into the town. With night falling Fairfax meant to wait for morning to make his assault, but at about 9 p.m. he realized that the Royalists were retreating, and gave the order to fall on. There followed a most unusual battle in the dark, in which the New Model beat the

Cavaliers from hedge to hedge into their barricades.

Hopton, in his account, accuses his men of deserting the barricades and retreating into the town in a panic, but if they did so, it was not without a fight. 'The dispute', Fairfax told Speaker Lenthall, 'continued long at push of pike and with butt-end of muskets.' Indeed, Hopton himself was wounded in the face with a pike. One, W.C.,[4] wrote: 'They maintained the barricadoes, lines and hedges, with as much resolution as could be expected, and had not our men gone on with extraordinary courage, they had been repulsed.' The Royalist cavalry tried to countercharge, clattering through the cobbled streets, and then, when the battle was at its height, the church blew up with a tremendous bang made by fifty barrels of powder stored there. Two hundred unhappy prisoners perished – had one of them been smoking his clay pipe, one wonders – and a number of Parliamentarian soldiers fell. Fairfax himself had one of his narrowest escapes here, for as he stood in the street a sheet of lead struck dead the man next to him.

When dawn broke the battle was lost and won. Of Hopton's army 600 were taken and 60 slain: 1,100 arms had been lost. The survivors were in full retreat for the Tamar, their wounded leader and the gallant Lord Capell holding the rearguard together.

Torrington was the death-knell of the Cornish foot, and before a month had passed the cavalry disbanded by the treaty of Truro. The officers of the old horse, lacking not only pay but horseshoes, had had enough. Of the generals only Hopton and Webb were for continuing the struggle. But the war in the West was not quite finished. At Pendennis Castle old Colonel John Arundell of Trerice and a band of diehards held out to the bitter end. Rushworth wrote to Lenthall on 13 April that the defenders had 'nothing but salt beef tainted, little quantity of bread and their wine almost spent'. On 27 June Arundell, John Digby and twelve others of the chief Cavaliers in the garrison wrote to Prince Charles in Jersey: 'Wee urge nothing for ourselves, nor the rest of your loyall servants here who are now poorly clothed, and sickly fedd upon bread and water.' By the end of July they were reduced to eating horseflesh. In August plague followed starvation and the men began to desert. One small boat-load of provisions got through, and the Cavaliers kept fires going all night to guide the relief ships which never came. Colonel Richard Fortescue, who commanded the besiegers knew the end was near when the besieged fired 200 great shot in three days. Such free expense of

powder argued that they did not expect to be able to hold out much longer.

On 15 August Arundell at last agreed to treat with Vice-Admiral William Batten and Colonel Fortescue. The treaty was signed next day 'condescended unto by me' wrote John Arundell at the foot. If Batten's surgeon, John Haslock, is to be believed, Digby and other officers meant to blow up the ordnance so that victors and vanquished should perish together. (There were ninety-four guns in the castle.) They were prevented by a mutiny of their own men.

On 17 August the garrison marched out with the honours of war, drums beating, colours flying and trumpets sounding. They actually demanded and received £500 for the care of their sick and wounded and to provide supplies for their journey. John Haslock found himself with 300 or 400 sick to look after, including 200 women and children. At the surrender the garrison comprised 154 officers and 732 soldiers. Some returned home, whilst a few preferred exile, and took ship for the Channel Islands or St Malo. Amongst these last was Sir Henry Killigrew, a Cornishman of the right Cavalier breed. He had been wounded by a splinter from a shot he had fired after the treaty was signed, and of this he died.

With the fall of Pendennis the war in the West was won. The New Model had meanwhile taken Oxford and its satellite fortresses as well as Exeter (13 April), Corfe Castle and Dunster Castle (April).

Its last exploit in the First Civil War was the taking of the

Marquis of Worcester's chief stronghold, Raglan Castle, which fell on 19 April 1646. The Marquis had kept his garrison in constant pay throughout the war, but as he had £24,000 per annum, this was not too difficult. He spent nearly £1 million for the cause. At stately Raglan he had entertained Charles after Naseby (3–22 July) when the King might have been better employed at the head of Goring's army. When I last visited Raglan I climbed to the top of the Tower of Gwent, and asked myself where the New Model would have planted its guns. On three sides the ground fell away from the old walls. On the fourth a herd of cows was grazing almost level with them. 'That', I thought 'will be the place', and went to see whether I could find any vestige of a battery. On the way I passed through a farmyard, where there were two ancient cannon-balls to be seen. They weighed them for me in a milk-pail: 29 and 18 lbs respectively. When I reached the cows I found that a flat platform had been made long ago, about 400 yards from the walls. And opposite the platform was the breach. Q.E.D. If you don't believe me go and see for yourself.

Notes

1. In a contemporary hand one William Cely, evidently a Parliamentarian, long since wrote these words on p. 320 of what in 1952 became my copy of Sprigg's *Anglia Rediviva*.
2. The ford where the road from Long Sutton to Langport crossed the Parret.
3. Mortally wounded afterwards at the siege of Bristol.
4. Possibly one of the clerks to Fairfax's secretary, John Rushworth, William Clarke.

CHAPTER 10

King Charles II's escape after Worcester, 1651

'The Miraculous Providence.'

The third day of September was an important one for Oliver Cromwell. On it he won the battle of Dunbar (1650), the battle of Worcester (1651) and on it, in 1658 he died.

'It is, for aught I know, a crowning mercy', wrote Cromwell in his Worcester despatch, and since he was now able to give up his military career, the battle certainly had something of a decisive nature. It would have been far more decisive had one of the casualties of the battle, 'or ta'en or slain', been his youthful opponent, King Charles II. Charles exposed himself fearlessly during the battle – not for nothing was he a grandson of Henri de Navarre. Had he fallen the head of the House of Stuart would have been that narrow-minded and pig-headed brother, who would eventually succeed him as James II. The prospects of the House of Cromwell would have been much enhanced! Had Charles been taken Oliver might have found himself in a quandary. Would he have made him follow his father to the scaffold? Or would he have lodged him in the Tower, or some more remote fortress? Who can say. Either course would have met with much opposition from the good people of England, whatever side they may have supported during the various campaigns of the Civil Wars. Maybe it was a real relief to Oliver Cromwell when he heard that the young man, Charles Stuart, had landed safely in France. That is not to say that the pursuit had been anything but relentless.

A visitor to Worcester can still see several places associated not only with the battle of 1651, but with the fight at Powick Bridge in 1642. On the south wall of the tower of Powick Church you can still see bullet splashes. These must be a legacy of 1651. We may imagine a stand of Scots pikemen arrayed in the churchyard, being peppered by Fleetwood's men moving in from Upton. The church on the low ridge called Ham Hill was an obvious outpost for the Royalists. The old bridge at Powick can still be seen, though it has now been bypassed. One can see easily enough, where a section was taken out by Montgomery's men in 1651, but the lane up which Sandys' men rode in 1642 is not so easy to locate, nor the field where Rupert was reposing himself in the September sun under a hawthorn tree. The 1642 fight at Powick Bridge was far from complicated. The Roundheads reached Powick Ham after a night march from Alcester via Upton.

The Earl of Essex, approaching Worcester from the south-east, had sent a strong detachment of horse and dragoons, under Colonel Edwin Sandys, to cut the city off from the west. They arrived in Powick Ham without any contact with their enemy. They raised their voices in a psalm, and then sent a forlorn hope across Powick Bridge as an advanced guard to protect the last stage of the march on Worcester. They then encountered the dragoons, who were covering the Prince's tired cavalry. A very simple clash followed, in which the Roundheads trying to deploy were driven back across, and in many cases into the River Teme. Many of the Roundheads did not draw rein till they reached Pershore – quite a gallop. Any victory raises the value, in terms of morale, of the troops who get the upper hand. Powick Bridge set the tone for Rupert's Horse.

Worcester Cathedral itself served as King Charles II's observation post in the 1651 battle. We may imagine him and a cluster of his chief officers watching the fluctuations of the Cromwellian tactics from that vantage point. It was no doubt from the summit of the tower that some alert Cavalier, reading the battle, made out Cromwell shifting his reserves across the River Severn, by means of his bridge of boats – or rather trows, the vessels of some 70 tons burthen, used until comparatively recent times to carry heavy loads, such as building materials, on the river.

Seeing Cromwell swing his reserves to the west bank, the King and the Duke of Hamilton led their men out of St Martin's and Sidbury gates, whilst the guns of the great Fort Royal thundered out their covering fire. The Cavaliers surged forward, driving the Roundheads back up Red Hill, and overrunning some of their guns.

Cromwell, with odds of two to one on his side, now brought his reserve back to the east bank. After a three-hour battle, the

King, having displayed 'an incomparable example of valour . . . by charging in person . . .' and setting a splendid example to the Highlanders who fought on with their musket butts after they had run out of ammunition, was driven back through Sidbury Gate. With them they carried the unlucky Duke of Hamilton, his leg shattered by a cannon-shot. He was borne to the Commandery, the King's headquarters, where he died. It is fortunate that the people of Worcester, the loyal city, conscious of their heritage have of late years rehabilitated the Commandery so that one may see it much as it was on that fatal day. All too much of the black and white city, which, under Colonel Henry Washington, sustained the siege of 1646, and saw the last cavalry charges on 3 September 1651, has vanished. The streets where the sixty-year-old Earl of Cleveland, hero of Cropredy Bridge and Second Newbury, charged to cover the King's escape, have been altered beyond recognition – in the name of progress. Still, it is easy enough to imagine Charles divesting himself of his armour and slipping away betwixt the quaint old houses. As dusk fell he and some sixty officers reached Kinver Heath. Their guide was lost, but Charles Gifford and his rustic servant, one Yates, guided the King through Stourbridge to Wardsley, where he downed a tankard of ale, before riding on, a crust in his hand.

As dawn broke the King reached the ruined monastery of Whiteladies, 50 miles from the scene of his defeat. Here was the home of the loyal if humble family of Penderel, five poor Catholic woodcutters, who lost no time in disguising the monarch with an old sweaty leather doublet, a green threadbare coat, a greasy steeple-crowned hat innocent of band or lining and a coarse noggen shirt. Portly, cheerful Lord Wilmot cut the royal locks with a knife, and made such a bad job of it that it had to be completed by Richard Penderel, with basin and shears.

The King spent a damp, rainy day in Spring Coppice, sustained towards midday by Elizabeth Yates, who brought him a blanket to sit upon, and a dish of milk, eggs and butter.

Charles, who had thought of making for London before the news of his defeat should get there, had now decided to make for Wales, and his plan was to make that night for Madeley, 10 miles to the west, where a Catholic gentleman of Penderel's acquaintance, might get him across the Severn. As dusk fell they left the coppice, and, crossiing a heath, came to Hobbal Grange, where Richard's widowed mother gave Charles her blessing and a hearty meal, and Francis Yates offered him his whole fortune –

Worcester Cathedral which served as King Charles II's observation post in the 1651 battle

thirty pieces of silver – of which the King, surprisingly considerate, took but ten.

It was a difficult journey, more absurd than dangerous, which took them to the house of sixty-nine-year-old Mr Francis Wolfe, who hid the King in a hayloft, and found him food, money, new shoes and stockings. The passage of the Severn proving too risky, the King and Penderel now set a course for Boscobel, and by three in the morning, after another adventurous night march, Charles was hidden in the woods between Whiteladies and Boscobel. Penderel went off to consult his brother and returned with Colonel William Careless, one of those who had played part in the last charge at Worcester, two days ago. There was news. Thanks to a Father Huddleston, Wilmot had found refuge at Moseley Hall, the home of a Catholic gentleman by the name of Thomas Whitgreave.

The three walked to the black and white lodge of Boscobel where Joan Penderel tended the monarch's blistered feet, and he breakfasted off bread and cheese and small beer. Then, at Careless' suggestion, they removed themselves to an old hollow oak, which overhung a busy road. From this vantage point they saw Roundhead soldiers searching the woods, whilst the Penderels by way of a diversion were 'peaking up and down' with their nut hooks. Charles dropped off, with his head in Careless' lap, and the Colonel's arm went to sleep too.

From Boscobel the King, mounted on an aged mill horse rode 8 miles to Madeley. Through the dark and stormy night, escorted by the five Penderel brothers and Yates, armed with stave and pistols, he made his way across Chillington Park and through the woods to Pendeford Old Mill, where his peasant lifeguard knelt to kiss his hand, and so parted.

Father Huddleston awaited his King in a grove in the corner of a field called the Moor. At Madeley the King, refreshed with sack, biscuits and a fresh shirt, declared that should God bless him with an army of resolute men, he would drive all the rogues out of his kingdom. He was certainly one of that breed that knows how to treat Triumph and Disaster!

Monday 8 September, after a comfortable night, Charles spent in a room over the porch, where he could survey the high road. Huddleston had three pupils, who were sent to keep a lookout, which, being boys, was very much to their taste. At supper the eldest sang out, 'Eat hard, boys, for we have been on the life-guard this day. . . .' As Mr Whitgreave commented it was 'more truly spoken than he was aware'.

On the afternoon of Tuesday 9 September there was an alarm. A company of militia was coming to search the house and arrest Mr Whitgreave for being at Worcester fight. The King was hidden in a priest-hole, and after a long altercation, Whitgreave's neighbours were able to convince the militia that he had not stirred from Moseley during the battle.

That King Charles died a Roman Catholic is not in doubt. It seems likely that his adherence to that faith dates from the time when his Catholic subjects protected him in his hour of trouble. In the evening the King told Huddleston that he knew he was a priest, 'and he needed not fear to own it, for if it pleased God to restore him to his kingdom, they should never more need privacies'. Huddleston showed the King his master's simple private oratory. It is easy to judge Charles by his more obvious attributes, a love for women and pleasure and so on. But the key to his skill in playing a poor hand, as he did throughout his reign, seems to lie in a perfectly genuine religious faith, which lay beneath an apparently frivolous character. This is, of course, not a judgement that will appeal to Roundheads. . . .

Colonel John Lane of Bentley, with two horses, arrived at midnight and waited in the orchard, and after a touching parting with Whitgreave, his aged mother and Father Huddleston, the King went on his way, promising them that if God were pleased to restore him 'he would not be unmindful'. The night was cold

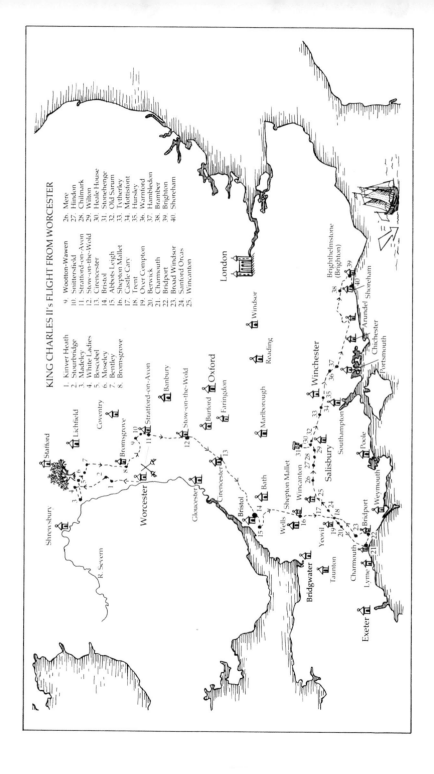

KING CHARLES II's FLIGHT FROM WORCESTER

1. Kinver Heath
2. Stourbridge
3. Madeley
4. White Ladies
5. Boscobel
6. Moseley
7. Bentley
8. Bromsgrove
9. Wootton-Wawen
10. Snitterfield
11. Stratford-on-Avon
12. Stow-on-the-Wold
13. Cirencester
14. Bristol
15. Abbots Leigh
16. Shepton Mallet
17. Castle Cary
18. Trent
19. Over Compton
20. Berwick
21. Charmouth
22. Bridport
23. Broad Windsor
24. Santord Orcas
25. Wincanton
26. Mere
27. Hindon
28. Chilmark
29. Wilton
30. Heale House
31. Stonehenge
32. Old Sarum
33. Tytherley
34. Mottistont
35. Hursley
36. Warnford
37. Hambledon
38. Bramber
39. Brighton
40. Shoreham

and Lane lent the King his cloak. They reached Bentley Park without incident.

Lane woke Charles at dawn, and gave him £20, and dressed him like a respectable farmer's son in a grey suit and cloak and a black steeple-crowned hat. They were practical folk some of these old Cavaliers.

The King, well briefed, brought the horses from the stables and awaited his mistress who was to ride pillion behind him.

Jane Lane, the Colonel's charming sister, mounted, trembling at the honour done her. (Her own mother was ignorant of it.) In Sir Arthur Bryant's felicitous phrase. 'For the next week she carried the Crown of England in her hands, and never was trust more bravely or delicately performed.'

So they set out and at the 'poor scattering village' of Bromsgrove the King's mare cast a shoe. The smith had not yet heard that the chief rogue, Charles Stuart, had been captured as yet. The King opined that 'if that rascal were taken he deserved to be hanged for bringing in the Scots, on which the smith replied with an oath that he spoke like an honest man'.

That afternoon they rode round the Forest of Arden and a little beyond Wootton-Wawen, an aged peasant warned them of soldiers on the Stratford road. Mr Petre, one of the party, who was ignorant of the King's identity, and who had once been beaten up by bibulous troopers, insisted upon avoiding them, so they made a detour by way of Snitterfield, only, upon entering Stratford-upon-Avon, to come face to face with the Roundhead troop. Charles saluted in a respectful fashion and the men opened right and left to let the travellers go by.

A 50-mile ride brought them that night to the house of John Tomes, a cousin of the Lanes, who lived at Long Marston.

On 11 September they rode through the Cotswolds, – Chipping Camden, Stow-on-the-Wold, Northleach and, at dusk, Cirencester.

On 12 September they reached Bristol. Charles knew the city well from 1645. With astonishing sang-froid he rode round Prince Rupert's fortifications, 'noting with surprise the many changes and improvements'. (Bryant) They made their way to Abbot's Leigh, where there were unexpected dangers. Dr George, a loquacious chaplain, who knew the King well, was there; and Pope the butler, had been a Royalist soldier. Miss Lane pretended her servant was sick of an ague. . . . Pope proved to be both loyal and intelligent. Hearing that Wilmot meant to visit the King, he warned the King that the servants were not to be trusted. He contrived to bring Wilmot to the royal bedchamber *sub nocte*.

The next move was to Trent near Sherborne, home of Colonel Frank Wyndham, the brave defender of Dunster Castle (1645–6), and brother-in-law of the King's nurse, who had taken a pot-shot at Old Noll at Bridgwater. Frank Wyndham yielded to no man in his cheerful loyalty. They journeyed via Shepton Mallet, and Castle Cary, where Lord Hertford's steward found them quarters for a night. At about 10 o'clock on 13 September they rode into Trent, where Wyndham and his young wife received them. 'Frank, Frank! How dost thou!' cried the King, who was evidently very far from being depressed by his misadventures.

At Trent Charles stayed for some days in a household of twenty people of whom only his host and his wife, their pretty little cousin Juliana Coningsby and the two loyal maids, Eleanor Withers and Joan Halsenoth, knew his identity.

It was here that Frank Wyndham told his sovereign how his father on his death-bed in 1636, had called his sons about him and told them they had lived in quiet days but must now prepare themselves for troublous times. 'I command you', he said as he expired, 'to honour and obey your sovereign, and, though the crown should hang upon a bush, I charge you forsake it not.' These words had had a very marked effect upon the gallant Colonel, who had held Dunster Castle so doggedly at the end of the First Civil War.

On the following Monday King Charles set off once more, this time with pretty Juliana Coningsby riding pillion. Wyndham was their guide. Wilmot, who scorned disguise, and Wyndham's servant, Peters, followed at a distance. By Over Compton and Berwick they went, crossing the Dorset Downs at Pilsdon Pen. Above Charmouth they met a Royalist merchant, named Ellesdon, who had chartered a vessel for them.

At dusk they rode down the steep hill into Charmouth and made their way to The Queen's Arms, which was packed with horse-copers from Lyme fair.

The wind stood fair for France and after supper Wyndham and Peters went to see how things were. At dawn the Colonel returned with bad news: the tide was out and no long-boat had come in. The Charmouth people were not incurious, and the blacksmith, who shod Wilmot's horse, was particularly so. But the King left for Bridport just in time, and one Captain Massey, with a troop of Roundhead militia, though zealous was not in time to prevent his departure.

Charles and his party reached Bridport to find the place full of redcoats, preparing for an amphibious operation: the invasion of Jersey.

Wyndham and Mistress Coningsby went into The George to order their supper, whilst the iron-nerved monarch shouldered his way through the soldiers in the stable yard. With some difficulty he evaded an ostler, who vowed he knew his face, and would drink with him. Juliana, who was evidently as bright as she was pretty, now spotted Peters in the street. From him they learned that Wilmot was in Bridport. He urged an immediate departure. His nonchalant conduct had shown that he was not one to take counsel of his fears. And so without delay they took the London road. A mile out of town, some inspiration made them take a lane northwards. No sooner had they done so than Massey's troop dashed past, going like the bats out of hell for Dorchester.

Night found the King and his party at a poor inn in the small village of Broadwindsor a few miles north of Bridport. Luckily the landlord was an old servant of the Wyndham family: both he and his wife were good Royalists and had suffered for the cause. They did not know how great an honour was being done them, but they took pains to make their guests comfortable. Remote though this country inn was a company of soldiers, marching to take part in the Jersey expedition, arrived at midnight and demanded quarters. They filled the house to overflowing, cutting off the King's attic. Fortunately for the Cavaliers the attention of the Roundhead soldiers was to a great extent focused upon a domestic drama. One of their doxies chose this moment to produce a baby upon the kitchen table. There was some controversy as to the child's upkeep. Was it the responsibility of the parish overseers, or of the military? The knot had not been untied by dawn, when the soldiers took to the road once more.

That morning Peters went to Lyme to see Ellesden, and returned to report that Mrs Limbry had locked her husband in his chamber rather than let him carry a dangerous cargo to France. The King and his party retreated to Trent and stayed there for another week. He spent much of his time boring holes in coins to make keepsakes for his hosts and their servants. Once he was enlivened by the sound of the church bells and the sight of disloyal peasants dancing around a bonfire. They had heard of his capture and death!

At dusk on Sunday 5 October Colonel Robert Phelips of Montacute appeared at Trent, having undertaken to charter a vessel at Chichester. Next day Charles bade the Wyndhams farewell and made a stage of 50 miles, the devoted Juliana Coningsby riding pillion once more, and Peters following. They rode by Sandford Orcas and Wincanton; to The George at Mere. Here they drank in the cellar, and the worthy innkeeper took a look at his incognito monarch saying: 'Thou lookest like an honest fellow. Here's a health to the King!' Charles, not unnaturally, was somewhat taken aback, whereupon his host demanded of Colonel Phelips what manner of Roundhead fellow he had brought with him. On in the afternoon via Hindon, Chilmark and Teffont, circling Salisbury Plain to Wilton. Here Charles said farewell to the gallant Juliana, and to Peters, and leaving the main road, Phelips and he made for Heale House, which they reached as night was falling.

Here the hostess, Mistress Hyde recognized the King at once and betrayed her loyalty by giving him two larks instead of one. One of the company that evening was the brave and learned Dr Henchman (1592–1675), Canon of Salisbury, who was to be

Bishop of London during the plague, when he set a noble example to his clergy by sticking firmly to his post.

Next day the King and Robert Phelips spent riding about upon Salisbury Plain and visiting Stonehenge. (The King succeeded in counting the stones twice alike.)

In the evening Henchman met them near Hale, and Phelips took his leave. The King spent the night in a secret hiding-hole.

On the night of 12/13 October Phelips returned with a horse for the King, and they rode through the night by Clarendon Park and Old Sarum, along the hills east of Salisbury and into Hampshire, by Tytherley and the woods of the Test Valley and so, by Mottisfont and Hursley to Twyford. On a high hill, called Old Winchester, above the little village of Warnford, they met Wilmot and Swan, his servant, and Colonel George Gunter of Racton, who was to prove a very efficient officer. Gunter revealed that there was a yeoman, who had married his sister, 'whose house stands privately and out of the way'.

'Let us go thither', said the King.

On they went over Broadhalfpenny Down, until they came to Mrs Symonds' house. Sir Arthur Bryant has described in his inimitable way, the scene that evening.

> That night was the pleasantest in all the King's travels. They sat down to supper at a round table, and, when the meal was almost over, the master of the house joined them. He, like an honest Cavalier, had been drinking in a tavern, and was filled with an hospitable desire to see all about him as merry as he. He settled down among his wife's guests, taking a stool by Charles, whose cropped hair and solemn aspect marked him out as a suitable object for conversion. Then, shaking his hand and mixing a bottle of strong waters in a tankard of beer, he called him Brother Roundhead and bade him drink deep. The scene is a delicious one – the wainscotted room, the firelight and the candles on the table, the faces of the hunted fugitives lit by the glow and the wine, and the hiccoughing host, half scared by the King's puritanical appearance, and wholly jovial. Whenever a bibulous oath escaped him, Charles was ready with the appropriate rebuke: 'Oh dear brother, this is a scape: swear not, I beseech you.' But the other was incorrigible. At ten o'clock, in order to let Charles escape to bed, Gounter suggested to his host that the Roundhead would be better away. Symonds gladly assented.

Next day the King, Wilmot, Gunter and Swan rode 30 miles through the New Forest, evading Colonel Herbert Morley, with his 'starched moustaches' whom they saw near Arundel Park. They crossed the River Arun at Houghton Bridge, and stopped for a draught at an ale-house. Gunter, like an old soldier, produced some of Mrs Symonds' neats' tongues – the unexpired portion of the day's rations. On by Chanctonbury Ring, then down through Bramber, which was full of heedless soldiers, who busy with their own affairs, made no attempt to prevent their crossing the Adur.

At Beeding they broke up, Charles and Wilmot went up Edburton Hill, and then cantered on, 9 miles to The George at the little fishing village of Brighthelmstone. Gunter and Swan arrived to hear the King's voice in the parlour: 'Here, Mr Barlow, I drink to you.' Truly, he was not the one to take his predicament too seriously.

Francis Mansel, a loyal merchant, found by Gunter, had negotiated with Nicholas Tattershall, master of a coal-brig to carry two fugitives to France for £60 down. These two came to supper at the George. When the meal was over, Tattershall told Mansel that he had not dealt fairly with him, for he had recognized the King. 'But', said he, 'be not troubled at it, for I think I do God and my country good service in preserving the King, and by the grace of God, I will venture my life and all for him, and set him safely on shore if I can in France.'

After supper while Charles stood alone by the fire, the

innkeeper, an old soldier of the Lifeguard, came in and began to talk. On a sudden he took the King's hand and kissed it, with: 'God bless you wheresoever you go; I do not doubt before I died to be a lord and my wife a lady!' Charles laughed and beat a retreat. His subjects could be embarassingly loyal.

At 2 a.m. Colonel Gunter called the King and Wilmot and led them to the creek at the mouth of the Adur, where the brig *Surprise* lay. At high water, about 7 o'clock, they set sail for Poole.

Gunter, who was not one to leave great matters to chance, followed all day, riding along the beach with the horses, and watching the distant sail.

Well out to sea, Tattershall told the King that the crew did not exactly understand what was up, whereupon Charles revealed that he and Wilmot were merchants, who were in debt, and promised them 25s. to spend on drink if they would support him in his efforts to talk the master into taking them to France! Human nature being what it is, they readily assented and, oddly enough, managed to bring Tattershall round to their viewpoint. At 5 p.m. with the Isle of Wight in sight to starboard the master put up his helm, and stood off for France with a following wind from the north. And so on Thursday 16 October, Charles, King of England, landed at Fécamp after six weeks of adventure and peril, such as few of his line have ever had to endure. He was sustained, we are still sustained, by the bravery and loyalty of the humbler folk, who have figured in this tale, and not least Jane Lane and Juliana Coningsby. Yet I suspect that were I once more to go upon such enterprises as came my way long ago with the Commandos, the one I would choose for a cool head in action would be Colonel George Gunter of Racton.

Appendix A

Nephew,

   First, I must congratulate with you for your good successes, assuring you that the things themselves are no more welcome to me that that you are the means. I know the importance of the supplying you with powder, for which I have taken all possible ways, having sent both to Ireland and Bristol. As from Oxford, this bearer is well satisfied that it is impossible to have [any] at present; but if he tell you that I can spare from hence, I leave you to judge, having but thirty-six left. But what I can get from Bristol (of which there is not much certainty, it being threatened to be besieged) you shall have.

['*Upon this break the pen changed.*']

['*Lord Culpepper not present at the writing of the letter or the consultation, as I suppose, but coming in after asked the King "If the letter was sent?" who said "Yes" – "Why, then," says he, "before God you are undone, for upon this peremptory order he will fight, whatever comes on't."* ']

   But now I must give the true state of my affairs, which, if their condition be such as enforces me to give you more *peremptory commands* than I would willingly do, you must not take it ill. If York be lost I shall esteem *my crown little less*; unless supported by your sudden march to me; and a miraculous conquest in the South, before the effects of their Northern power can be found here. *But if* York be relieved, and *you beat the rebels' army* of both kingdoms, which are before it; then (*but otherwise not*)* [* 'This parenthesis inserted by the Lord Wilmot.'] I may possibly make a shift (upon the defensive) to spin out time until you come to assist me. Wherefore I *command and conjure you,* by the duty and affection which I know you bear me, that all new enterprises laid aside, you immediately march, according to your first intention, with all your force to the relief of York. But if that be either lost, or have freed themselves from the besiegers, or that, for want of powder, you cannot undertake that work, that you immediately march with your whole strength, directly to Worcester, to assist me and my army; without which, or your having relieved York by beating the Scots, all the successes you can afterwards have must infallibly be useless unto me. You may believe that nothing but an extreme necessity could make me write thus unto you; wherefore, in this case, I can no ways doubt of your punctual compliance with

Your loving uncle and most faithful friend,

CHARLES R.

P.S. – I commanded this Bearer to speak to you concerning [Sir William] Vavasour.

Ticknell [Tickenhill] June 14th, 1644.

Appendix B

Marston Moor order of battle

	Royalists		
	Horse	*Foot*	*Total*
Goring	2,100–2,400	500	2,600– 2,900
Centre and Reserve	1,300–1,600	1,100	12,300–12,600
Byron	2,600–2,700	500	3,100– 3,200
	6,000–6,700	12,000	18,000–18,700

	Allies			
	Horse	*Dragoons*	*Foot*	*Total*
T. Fairfax and Eglington	3,000	500	600	4,100
Centre	–	–	17,800–18,800	17,800–18,800
Cromwell and Leslie	4,700	500	600	5,800
	7,700	1,000	19,000–20,000	27,000–28,700

The numbers are, of course, approximate, and it may be that those of the Allies, in particular, are too strong, wastage at the siege of York is difficult to estimate.

Select Bibliography

(Place of publication London, unless otherwise stated)

Chapter 1

Gardiner, S. R., *History of the Great Civil War, 1642–9* (1893).
Wedgwood, C. V., *The King's Peace* (1955).
Wedgwood, C. V., *The King's War* (1958).

Chapter 2

Atkyns, Richard and Gwyn, John, *Military Memoirs*. Ed. Brigadier Peter Young and Norman Tucker (1967).
Dictionary of National Biography. Oxford Univ. Press.
Heath-Agnew, E., *Roundhead to Royalist*. Hereford, 1977.
Hopton, Lord, *Bellum Civile*. Ed. Charles E. H. Chadwyck-Healey, Somerset Record Society (1902).
Hutchinson, Lucy, *Memoirs of the Life of Colonel John Hutchinson*. Ed. C. H. Firth (1885).
Iter Carolinum (1660).
Ludlow, Edmund, *The Memoirs of Edmund Ludlow*. Ed. C. H. Firth, Oxford (1894)
Morrah, Patrick, *Prince Rupert of the Rhine* (1976).
Slingsby, Sir Henry, *The Diary of Sir Henry Slingsby*. Ed. Rev. Daniel Parsons (1836).
Sprigg, Joshua, *Anglia Rediviva*.
Symonds, Richard, *The Diary of Richard Symonds*. Ed. C. E. Long, Camden Society, Vol. 74 (1859).

Wharton, Sergeant Nehemiah, 'Letters'. Ed. Sir Henry Ellis, *Archaeologia*, Vol. XXV (1853).

Chapter 3

Clark, Andrew (ed.), *The Life and Times of Anthony Wood, Antiquary of Oxford, 1632–1694, Described by Himself.* Vol. I: 1632–1663. Oxford (1891).
Toynbee, Margaret and Young, Peter, *Strangers in Oxford*. London and Chichester (1973).
Varley, F. J., *The Siege of Oxford*. Oxford (1932).

Chapter 4

Firth, C. H., *Cromwell's Army* (1902).

Collections

H.M. Tower of London.
Littlecote House.

Chapter 5

Adair, Dr John, *Cheriton 1644. The Campaign and the Battle*. Kineton (1973).
Burne, Lieutenant-Colonel A. H., *Battlefields of England* (1950). Chapters on Edgehill, First Newbury, Marston Moor, Second Newbury and Naseby.
Burne, Lieutenant-Colonel A. H., *More Battlefields of England* (1952), Chapters on Lansdown, Roundway Down, Cheriton and Langport.
Hopton, Lord, *Bellum Civile*. Ed. Charles E. H. Chadwyck-Healey, Somerset Record Society (1902). Includes Braddock Down, Launceston, Stratton, Lansdown and Cheriton.
Toynbee, Margaret and Young, Brigadier Peter, *Cropredy Bridge 1644: The Campaign and the Battle*. Kineton (1970).
Young, Brigadier Peter, *Edgehill, 1642. The Campaign and the Battle*. Kineton (1967).

Chapter 6

Duffy, Christopher, *Siege Warfare. The Fortress in the Early Modern World, 1494–1660*. London and Henly (1979).

Ross, Lieutenant-Colonel W. G., 'Military engineering during the Great Civil War, 1642–49', *Professional Papers of the Corps of Royal Engineers*, Chatham (1888).

Royal Commission on Historical Monuments, England, *Newark on Trent: The Civil War Siegeworks* (1964).

Young, Peter and Emberton, Wilfred, *Sieges of the Great Civil War, 1642–1646* (1978).

Chapter 7

Coate, Mary, *Cornwall in the Civil War and Interregnum 1642–46*, 2nd ed. Truro (1963).

Hopton, Lord, *Bellum Civile*. Ed. Charles E. H. Chadwyck-Healey, Somerset Record Society (1902).

Chapter 8

Wenham, L. P., *The Great and Close Siege of York*. Kineton (1970).

Young, Brigadier Peter, *Marston Moor 1644: The Campaign and the Battle*. Kineton (1970).

Chapter 9

Coate, Mary, *Cornwall in the Great Civil War and Interregnum, 1642–46*. 2nd edn., Truro (1963).

Sprigg, Joshua, *Anglia Rediviva; England's Recovery*. London (1647).

Chapter 10

Bryant, Arthur, *King Charles II* (1931).

Index